SPACE AND SOCIETY 6
PRACTICAL
APPROACHES

SPACE AND SOCIETY 6

PRACTICAL APPROACHES

Andrew Kirby and David Lambert

LONGMAN

LONGMAN GROUP LIMITED
*Longman House, Burnt Mill, Harlow, Essex CM20 2JE, England
and Associated Companies throughout the World*

First published 1985
ISBN 0 582 35352 1

Set in 10/11pt Baskerville, Linotron 202

*Published by Longman Singapore Publishers (Pte) Ltd
Printed in Singapore*

Contents

Acknowledgements

We are grateful to the following for permission to reproduce copyright material:

Guardian Newspapers Limited for the article 'Census shows drift out of towns' by Gareth Parry from *The Guardian* Tuesday 30/6/81 and Hertfordshire Mercury and County Press for the article 'Last orders at The Old Fox' from *Hertfordshire Mercury* 25/7/80.

We are grateful to the following for permission to reproduce photographs:

Camera Press, photo Colin Davey, page 83; Christian Frenzel, pages 82 and 85; Henry Grant, page 86; Office of Population Censuses and Surveys, Crown copyright, reproduced with the permission of Her Majesty's Stationery Office, page 84.

Preface

To the teacher

Aims

This series is designed for use within the sixth form as a back-up to the now familiar texts such as Tidswell's *Pattern and Process in Human Geography*, Bradford and Kent's *Human Geography* and Haggett's *Modern Synthesis*. We have designed the books as 'readers', that is, free-standing volumes that elaborate on particular topics, fleshing out the bare bones introduced within the textbook by presenting extracts from original sources and illustrative exercises. The latter are particularly important, as the emphasis throughout the series is upon the practical application of ideas, models and theories, rather than the abstract discussion of such deductive concepts. In this sense, the aim is to use the student's existing experiences of the 'real world' as a foundation for investigation, in order that these can be channelled into a systematic understanding of basic geographic principles.

Organisation

This book can be used in three ways. It is intended for use as a whole; in other words, the student should be able to use both the practical material and the original extracts in approaching a particular topic. In some instances, however, this may not be required. In such cases, it should be possible to use the practical examples alone, or if required, the published extracts as reference material.

To the student

This book is one of a series of geography 'readers'. This means that the aim of the series is not to provide a complete source of facts and information for your sixth-form course; instead the intention is to provide a firm grounding in some of the fundamental ideas within the subject.

You should aim to read the volumes in the series as a back-up to your course. If you have problems in understanding some sections, discuss them with your teacher. Many of the ideas will become clearer as you work through the examples.

1
Local investigator

1.1 The scope of local investigation and this book

In books 1–5 in this series *Space and Society* we have identified a number of themes or issues which either have great importance to geography as an academic discipline (*The Region*; *Interaction*) or are subject matters which are particularly suitable to analyse from the geographical perspective (*Urban Systems*; *The City*). Throughout the series we have drawn heavily from the work of professional geographers both to introduce ideas and arguments, and also to illustrate them more fully through exercises. Wherever possible you have been asked to think about and use your own local area, and several of the exercises have been firmly based in this context. It is in order to develop this in more detail that this volume is written; the aim is really to give some general guidelines on how to set up a larger scale local geographical investigation that will yield satisfactory and, possibly, quite original results. There is, of course, no definitive formula that can be followed, step by step, in conducting a piece of geographic research. There are certain rules and modes of analysis that can be adopted and, more important, pitfalls that must be avoided. But the actual methodology that is used depends very largely on the subject-matter and what the precise aims of the investigation are. Thus, the text is illustrated with examples of actual local projects, some of which were attempted by sixth formers.

Fieldwork has always been a central part of geography; indeed in the early days, before geography was a university or a school subject, the real job of the geographer was to find out about the globe which, amongst other things, meant exploring uncharted areas of the world. Books would be written and maps drawn describing these hitherto unknown regions. When geography began to be *taught* in the early part of the twentieth century, an almost essential part of the kitbag of the student was a pair of stout shoes; in a subject concerned with the world as it is – rather than how it used to be in the past, for example – a student would have felt less than satisfied not getting out and about. After all, seeing is believing! (Or so it is often tempting to suppose.) This kind of fieldwork, which we may describe as largely 'looking', is still vitally important; how much easier it is to properly appreciate coastal landforms, or the nature of a New Town, after having seen them! However, there is a distinction between this kind of fieldwork and that which we will call 'local investigation'. After all you 'know' your local area; that is to say, you recognise it when you see it.

Local investigation utilises several skills – amongst them *observation* rather than just looking – in order to reveal some aspect of the local geography that might not be immediately apparent; that is to say, something beyond a superficial 'knowing' (although local knowledge, of course, may help considerably in this task, especially in the initial stages of the investigation).

The scope of this particular book should be carefully noted. It is *not* intended to be a manual of the various useful techniques of data collection, description and analysis that the local investigator may well need. It does not contain lists of formulae or data sheets. It *is* written with these specific aims: a) to help each individual student to prepare him or herself; b) to help the student select a suitable project topic; c) to help the student devise his or her own method; d) to guide the student toward useful sources of data and other information; e) to point out pitfalls that can be avoided. It may be, however, that the examples used in the text will stimulate ideas for your project.

An important introductory point concerns scale. *Local* investigation is not a very precise measure of the scale of a possible project and, in fact, it would be unnecessarily restricting to suggest some sort of exact spatial dimensions to a 'local' project. However, it is worth noting that bigger is not necessarily better. Students are not the most mobile members of society in any case, and, with very real additional time and cost constraints, it is easy to 'bite off more than you can chew'.

The most important thing is to be precise and clear about what aspect you wish to pursue and *then* draw the boundary around your field area, which may be a single small town, or a single neighbourhood within a town, or even a single feature within a town such as a factory. Indeed the very aim of your project might be to define the boundary, as in the mapping of the sphere of influence of a shopping street. More will be said about scale in section 2.4.

To summarise, the following pages are written to provide a vital framework in which the student can work. Essentially, the message is to think and plan ahead; each stage of the local investigation must be thought out carefully before the major field work or data collection is undertaken. The ill-thought-out local investigation reminds us of the aimless traveller: if you don't know which way you are heading, you cannot be sure of your destination. Good projects are completed by students who know what they wish to find

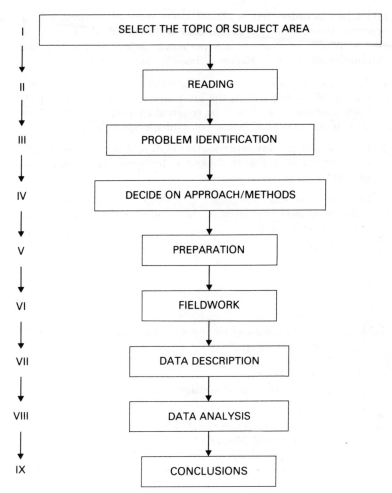

I — SELECT THE TOPIC OR SUBJECT AREA

II — READING

III — PROBLEM IDENTIFICATION

IV — DECIDE ON APPROACH/METHODS

V — PREPARATION

VI — FIELDWORK

VII — DATA DESCRIPTION

VIII — DATA ANALYSIS

IX — CONCLUSIONS

Figure 1.1   Step-by-step approach to individual project work

out about their local environment and systematically devise a
method which enables them to work toward a clear conclusion.

Figure 1.1 illustrates a simple step-by-step approach to the planning of a piece of local research. It will be noted that the actual
'fieldwork' element does not occur until *stage VI* in the diagram and
that a great deal of work is to be done before this stage. Apart from
any other considerations, this is important in the interests of effi-
ciency; there is nothing more frustrating and ultimately damaging
to the finished product than realising when out 'in the field' that
you have not been collecting data on a vitally important aspect of
the study! Figure 1.1 is of general applicability for a wide range of

topics but in order that is should make more of an impact in a practical sense, table 1.1 should also be consulted which expands each step with reference to a hypothetical project on housing and externality effects (see chapter 2, book 2, 'Interaction').

1. After studying table 1.1, attempt to write a summary in approximately 100 words stating the aims and methods of the project. Such a summary may well be required by your teacher or even an external examiner before you embark upon the project.

2. Can you identify any other sources of data that might be readily obtainable and of potential use for this particular hypothetical project?

3. Do you think that this study is realistic? Can you propose a different method to investigate the same or similar topic (i.e. the effect of externalities and externality 'fields' in the local environment)?

Table 1.1   *A brief summary of the step-by-step approach to an individual study of Housing.*

I   SELECT TOPIC
Urban geography; housing.

II   READING
Several texts recommended by teacher
Geographical Magazine
Other specialised articles if available
Specialised local material from planning department or library

III   PROBLEM INDENTIFICATION
After discussion with teacher, the specific area of local study is identified as house-price variation. What are the explanatory factors? More specifically, does the proximity of certain land-uses, such as a factory or park, have any negative or positive impact on house price? If so, can the spatial extent of the impact be measured?

IV   APPROACH AND METHODS
Estate agents to be source of house-price data. Estate agents interviewed to ascertain how house price valuations are made; this may require a standard format of questions.

V   PREPARATION
Require street plan with large scale to accurately locate houses and other land-uses.
Find out all local estate agents.
Reconnoitre town; do I need to study whole town or part of town?
Are there any problems I can predict, and therefore avoid?

VI   FIELDWORK
Fieldwork – completed in a 4-day period.

VII   DATA DESCRIPTION
Attempt to standardise data.
Find averages and variation of standardised data.
Maps to show location of the land-uses under examination and individual houses.

VIII   DATA ANALYSIS
Does the data *need* testing statistically? Or is cartographic evidence enough to enable you to draw conclusions?

IX   CONCLUSIONS
Are my conclusions justified? Are they weak in any way? How could this study be taken further of improved?

Discussion

It is possible that *rateable values* of properties might be obtained and used in conjunction with *house prices*. However the rateable value of a house does not necessarily take into account the property's location quite so sharply as the market value of the house. A short 'pilot' study may reveal whether this is so or not; indeed one of the aims of the project might be to determine whether this is so. Alternatively, it may be thought that the whole approach of the project outlined in table 1.1 will not be very productive. There are other ways to measure externality fields and perhaps interviewing residents in order to ascertain their feelings about certain factories or parks may be thought better.

This is not intended as a 'template' for a local investigation. It is a hypothetical example which should illustrate the importance of proper thought and preparation that is required in the launching of your local project. Selecting a topic or title can sometimes prove the most difficult activity in the whole process, and the remainder of this chapter discusses different types of project that may be considered.

1.2 Testing a known idea or theory

The results of all academic investigation require careful verification
before they can be accepted as being reliable. Sometimes this is
immensely difficult to achieve and in such cases the theory is
perhaps accepted on trust, at least until a better one is presented,
because it sounds reasonable and seems to make sense. We can
examine this argument further with special reference to Geography.
Geography is the social science which specifically focuses on the
spatial viewpoint, and a theory or idea that is demonstrated to work
in one region, city or locality may not necessarily be expected to
work elsewhere. Indeed it may be of interest to determine just that;
that is, whether the theory developed in one area can be applied
to other areas, or even universally.

To illustrate this point, we may think of the example of trade
areas around towns. (See figure 3.3 in book 3, *'Urban System'*). This
is an instance of a universally accepted idea and would be relatively
straightforward to construct a similar map for a town near you;
indeed transport engineers and the managers of shopping centres
often do conduct surveys to determine trade areas for it is useful
information to them. An important point to note is that, although
the idea is of universal applicability, all trade areas are not *identical*.
In fact it would be more accurate to say that they are 'unique', the
size and shape of the trade area being dependent upon local
circumstances of public transport provision, the road network and
so on.

Thus, one kind of local research project that may be undertaken
by the sixth-form student is one that takes an established idea or
theory and attempts to reproduce it in the local area, or test its
applicability.

Of course, this is not necessarily as easy or as straightforward
as it might seem at first glance. The fundamental 'rules' implied
at the end of previous section (1.1) still apply. You might be quite
clear about what you hope to achieve, but you still have to think
out each stage taking special care not to 'cheat' and simply end up
with contrived results. The following example may help to illustrate
what we mean:

Here we have a diagram that summarises the results of some
research on the trade areas of individual stores in an urban area.
Brennan's Law states that the trade area or catchment area of an
urban store 'takes the form of a semi-circle on the side of the shop
away from the centre of the town'. This is illustrated in the diagram
and you will observe that shopper S, for example, will probably
shop at B rather than C, even though the latter is nearer to the
residential location of S.

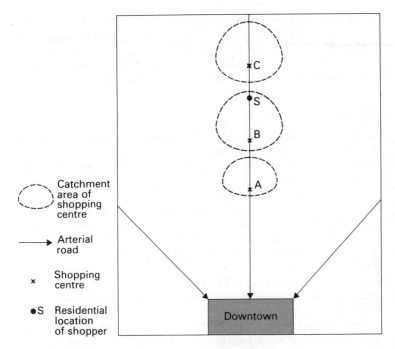

Figure 1.2 'Brennan's Law for shopping behaviour'

The objective of this piece of research was, of course, to investigate shopping behaviour, and more specifically the way shoppers *perceive* the location of shops in their local environment. Shoppers carry with them mental maps of their neighbourhoods and the wider urban area, and this research indicates that there is a tendency for shoppers to perceive distances to points away from the town centre as greater than those to points located in the direction of the town centre. It is as if shoppers have a natural bias toward locations near the city centre.

Thus, we have the results of research completed well over a decade ago and it is just the kind of idea or theory that could form the basis of a hypothesis for an individual local studies project. Consider the following questions:

1. Would it be feasible to attempt to test this particular hypothesis in *your* particular local area? Describe the kind of area for which Brennan's Law might be applicable.

2. Imagine that you are undertaking an investigation to test Brennan's Law. We can assume you have covered items I, II and III on figure 1.1. Suggest how you would approach the project and what methods you might employ (item IV in figure 1.1).

3. Imagine that you have conducted your fieldwork and your results contradict Brennan's Law. In this situation imaginative thought is sometimes necessary in order to suggest explanations. Try to think of one sound reason why shoppers might *not* have a natural bias toward shops in the direction of the town centre.

Discussion

Clearly, this is not the kind of study that can be easily carried out in a rural area. The ideal area would be a sizeable town which contains a number of shopping points or streets away from the Central Business District. Without going into details, this kind of project is the kind that requires a simple household questionnaire survey to determine individual shopping habits, the location of the sampled households being carefully marked on a large-scale map, as well as individual shops named by respondents. An alternative approach would be to conduct the questionnaire outside shops that you have previously identified. (More is said about questionnaire techniques in section 3.3.) The results of your study are naturally unforeseeable, but it is quite possible that they would not support Brennan's Law. In fact, this outcome is quite likely in the case of a town with a large, accessible 'Outer Business District' with good parking facilities; suburban hypermarkets are now a major attraction away from the central area of towns, particularly in the case of non-specialised shopping such as the weekly food shopping.

1.3 Conducting parallel work

Your classwork or reading may suggest fieldwork projects of a slightly different variety. The previous section discussed ideas that could be *tested* for their validity in your local environment. In this section we shall see an example of a piece of research, the results of which do not necessarily lend themselves to being 'tested' so much as suggesting work of a parallel nature that could be attempted in your local area.

The example in the previous section reminded us that it is how individuals perceive their environment that often helps explain how they behave. Figure 1.3 follows the same broad theme as it shows the results of many individuals' perception of their neighbourhoods within part of the city of Cambridge. In other words, it shows the boundaries that people would draw around the local area that they would call 'home territory'. (See figure 3.2 in book 1, *The Region*,) for a further example and for a wider discussion of this theme.)

The issue of neighbourhoods within towns is a large and complex one and it would be a mistake to attempt a project that had aims

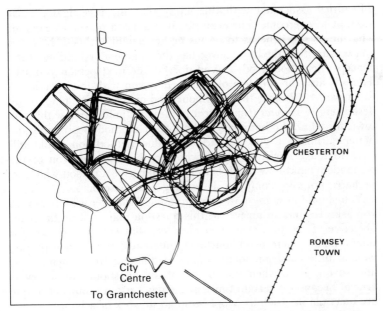

CHESTERTON

ROMSEY
TOWN

City
Centre
To Grantchester

Figure 1.3   An aggregate map of perceived neighbourhoods in Cambridge

that were too ambitious. However, an attempt to work on a theme similar to the one shown in figure 1.3 may be rewarding. Before embarking on such a project, though, some creative thought is, of course, required:

1. Figure 1.3 shows the mapped results of a neighbourhood perception study. The map has been based upon information collected from the field. Outline what you think the information was and in what form it was collected.

2. Describe how you would set about obtaining this information; specifically what we mean here is *who* you would ask, and *where* you would conduct the fieldwork?

3. What kind of area would be most suitable for this type of project? Do you think it could be adapted in any way to suit an urban fringe or even rural area?

Discussion

This study aims to find out information concerning the mental maps of individuals and so, clearly, people have to be asked. Therefore, a questionnaire seems appropriate. However, there are particular difficulties associated with this study that the investigator must attempt to overcome. For example, if you ask a person at random what he or she believes to be his or her neighbourhood, how can you be sure that the interviewee has the same understanding of the concept 'neighbourhood' as you do? Or the next person you ask? There is also the problem of exactly how you wish the interviewee to answer; by *drawing* the neighbourhood on an outline map, or by describing it in *words* using street names and landmarks within the town to define the boundary? The former method is probably the better, although if you were to adopt this method you would still have to make decisions about who did the drawing (you or the respondent) and how much help you would give a person who was, perhaps, not very confident at reading your base-map.

You should attempt to decide for yourself whether it matters who you ask. To find an answer to this question may well be the main objective of the project as you may feel that younger age groups might define their neigbhourhood differently from older people, women different from men, employed different from unemployed and so on. If so, then the timing of the questionnaire survey is crucial because at certain times of the day certain groups of people are unavailable, such as people who go to work or school.

Many local projects will contain practical problems which have to be tackled, such as those we have outlined for this particular example. It is how thoroughly these problems are tackled that will often determine how successful the finished piece of work is.

1.4 The application of a tried and tested technique

In the previous two sections we have briefly discussed practical projects which have been stimulated by the objective of a concrete goal. In both cases the *method* involved is the subject of much thought and has to be devised; the objective is known and the investigator must construct his or her own route toward this, overcoming the problems of bias, and others, on the way.

An alternative approach to practical geography may be to use a method or technique that has already been utilised by professional geographers or planners and has been widely accepted as fair and reliable. On some occasions, the method can be adapted or adjusted, maybe to suit local conditions, but because the method is 'second hand' the creativity in such a study does not lie here but elsewhere. In other words, the investigator must be sure that the method or technique selected is suitable for the project that it is to be used for. It is also the skill with which the investigator interprets and assesses the results that determines how successful the project will be.

We can illustrate this kind of study with reference, once again, to urban areas. One field of investigation concerns the environmental quality of housing areas and how this varies spatially within the town. This is of interest to the residents themselves, of course, as the 'attractiveness' of housing districts certainly plays a part in influencing the residential location decisions of individuals as well as influencing house prices. Environmental quality is also of interest to town planners who on occasion must advise on policy towards urban renewal or improvement and so on, and it is really a result of this interest in housing that techniques have been devised to measure environmental quality.

Such techniques have not been easy to design. They normally consist of a classification of features and facilities in the housing landscape, each of which must be given a score or penalty points according to a pre-determined scale of values. The field investigator uses the field-survey sheet (containing the classification and scoring system) to assess the overall quality of a number of survey points within the town. Table 1.2 gives an example of a field-survey sheet which would give each survey point an overall score of between 0 and 100. The greater the score the poorer is the quality of the environment, and very large scores (say, over 50) denote areas in serious need of attention and possible redevelopment.

Table 1.2   Environmental standards for a primary residential area

Factor	Points sub-factor	Score factor
Traffic		
0. Full separation of pedestrain and normal residential traffic	0	
1. Very limited intrusion of through traffic. . .	1–2	
2. Some – substantial intrusion of through traffic . . .	3–8	
3. Excessive intrusion of through traffic . . .	9–11	11
Non-conforming uses (within or nearby)		
0. Exclusively residential uses . . .	0	
1. Limited infiltration . . . non-conforming uses	1–2	
2. Some substantial infiltration of . . . non-conforming uses	3–7	
3. Excessive infiltration of . . . non-conforming uses	8–9	9

Factor	Points sub-factor	Score factor
Rateable value (broad assessment of housing conditions)		
0. More than £100 average	0	
1. £56–100 average	3	
2. £31–£56 average	6	
3. £23–30 average	7	
4. £0–£22 average	9	9
Landscaping/visual quality		
0. Mature, good quality trees...and well-kept grassed spaces	0–1	
1. Insufficient poor quality trees... and/or unkempt grassed spaces	2–5	
2. Total, or almost total, lack of trees/grassed spaces	6–7	7
Access to primary school		
0. Primary school within 5 minutes' walking distance	0	
1. Primary school 5–10 minutes' walking distance ...	2	
2. Primary school more than 10 minutes' walking distance ...	5	
3. Primary school more than 10 minutes' walking distance but involving main road crossing(s)	7	7
Access to other facilities (shops, pub, doctor)		
0. Shops, pub and doctor all within 5 minutes' walking distance	0	
1. Shops only within 5 minutes' walking distance	2	
2. Pub and doctor within 5 minutes' walking distance	4	
3. Doctor or pub within 5 minutes' walking distance ...		
4. No facilities within 5 minutes' walking distance	6	6

Factor	Points sub-factor	Score factor
Access to children's playground		
0. Playground within 2 minutes' walking distance . . .	0	
1. Playground within 2 minutes' walking distance but involving main road crossing(s)	2	
2. Playground 2–4 minutes' walking distance . . .	3	
3. Playground 2–4 minutes' walking distance but involving main road crossing(s)	5	
4. No playground within 4 minutes' walking distance	6	6
Garaging/parking provision		
0. Full provision of garaging/parking facilities	0	
1. 75%–95% provision of garaging/parking facilities	1	
2. 50%–74% provision of garaging/parking facilities . . .	2	
3. 25%–49% provision of garaging/parking facilities . . .	4	
4. 0%–24% provision of garaging/parking facilities . . .	6	6
Townscape/visual quality		
0. Harmonious, attractive arrangement of . . . elements . . .	0	
1. Some discordance or drabness within the . . . elements	1–3	
2. Excessive discordance or drabness within the . . . elements	4–5	5
Access to park		
0. Park . . . within 5 minutes' walking distance . . .	0	
1. Park . . . within 5 minutes' walking distance but involving main road crossing(s)	1	

Factor	Points sub-factor	Score factor
2. Park . . . 5–10 minutes' walking distance	2	
3. Park . . . 5–10 minutes' walking distance but involving main road crossing(s)	4	
4. No park within 10 minutes' walking distance	5	5
Access to public transportation		
0. Public transport route within 3 minutes walking distance . . .	0	
1. Public transport route 3–5 minutes' walking distance	2	
2. No public transport route within 5 minutes' walking distance	5	5
Microclimate		
0. No discomfort from microclimatic factors	0	
1. Some discomfort from microclimatic factors, i.e. which minor improvements, e.g. tree-planting could alleviate	1–2	
2. Excessive discomfort from microclimatic factors	3–4	4
Garden provision		
0. Full provision of adequate gardens or communal	0	
1. Insufficient provision of adequate or inadequate gardens	1–2	
2. Excessive lack of gardens . . .	3–4	4
Appearance of traffic structures/uses		
0. No depreciation in visual quality . . . by traffic structures/uses	0	
1. Some depreciation in visual quality	1–2	
2. Excessive depreciation	3	3

Source: J. Hancock, 1980

After examining table 1.2 the main purpose of a detailed assessment sheet will possibly be clear already. Without a strict system to guide the field investigator, the problem of subjectivity would be ruinous; surveys of the same area conducted by different people would produce wildly differing results because the observers would give different weightings to the various facilities and features in the district.

1. Illustrate, by giving one example from the field-survey sheet in table 1.2, how the assessment method attempts to cut out subjectivity and scores housing areas objectively. Is there still a subjective element in the sheet? If so, is it justified?

2. Describe how you would use the sheet in the field. Would you, for example, assess an area from just one fixed point or would you suggest that walking around an area would be preferable? How large an area of housing can be suitably assessed by a single score?

3. Suggest how the results of an investigation using the field-survey sheet could be presented cartographically. Do your suggestions have any implications for the fieldwork?

Discussion

The field-survey sheet attempts to be all-inclusive and in doing so subjectivity is reduced substantially. Suburban areas which may be leafy, clean and quiet and, therefore, score few penalty points on appearance, will score heavily (badly) on access and public transportation; inner city areas will score the reverse. The subjectivity that remains is associated with the interpretation by the field investigator of words like 'excessive' or 'mature', but it would be unreasonable not to have this kind of flexibility and surveys that did ignore this little bit of latitude would probably be so general as to be of little use.

Some cartographic techniques are briefly discussed in chapter 4 of this book. If we imagine that an isoline map of environmental quality scores is the most desirable technique then we have to be sure that we observe and record an adequate number of survey points to make the construction of such a map possible. In any case, some sort of mapped presentation would seem to be desirable in a project such as this and every effort needs to be made to ensure that individual scores are representative. For this reason, it is suggested that small housing *areas* (of, say 50 metres × 50 metres) be assessed rather than simply selected *points* or streets within the town.

A final point concerning the particular example selected here is that it is clearly a complicated and time consuming procedure. Unless a student shows unusual dedication to the task, this is undoubtedly the type of field project that is better suited to teamwork in order to guarantee adequate coverage of the town under investigation.

1.5 A novel idea

So far we have discussed projects that have their roots in ideas or techniques that might be found in text books and other geographical literature. There is no reason, however, why a sound and interesting fieldwork project cannot be stimulated by other sources. There might be a particular feature in your local surroundings that could merit quite original geographical study. The following example will illustrate this more clearly.

Figure 1.4 shows a short newspaper article taken from the *Hertfordshire Mercury* which is an account of the demise of an old public house, The Fox, in the village of Meesden in East Hertfordshire. Most of East Hertfordshire is within 40 miles of London and yet the character of the district is very 'rural'. Rurality is a difficult concept to define precisely and there is no space here to discuss it fully except to say that many people who live in East Hertfordshire *feel* rural and would classify themselves as rural dwellers. One of the reasons for this is lack of service provision and the decline in some services as illustrated by the newspaper article. Meesden, it should also be noted, has no shop or post office either. School students, of course, may feel the effects of the lack of facilities more than other groups; the shortage of social amenities and the absence of public transport perhaps having a particularly strong impact. It is possible that the experience illustrated by the article could encourage a substantial practical project for the student living in Meesden or in a nearby community.

1. East Hertfordshire has been very briefly described above. Propose three practical field investigations that may suggest themselves from the article (figure 1.4).

2. For each suggestion, briefly describe how the study might be attempted. What information would need to be collected? How would you go about collecting it and what methods would you use?

Discussion

Book 2 in this series, 'Interaction', could be usefully consulted in this context. Chapter 1 discusses mobility and the 'action spaces'

July 25, 1980

Last orders at the old Fox

Village pub to be sold

EAST HERTS is to lose one of its oldest public houses— the Fox at Meesden— which is to be sold without the licence when licensee Mrs Violet Prosser and her husband, Tom, pull their last pints in two weeks' time.

Violet took over as licensee nearly 15 years ago, while Welsh-born Tom, as a self-employed painter and decorator, has always carried on his own job and helped at the pub in the evenings and at weekends.

It was their first venture into the licensing trade— and also the first time they had lived in the country.

The couple were brought up in Enfield—where Violet was born—and lived there until they moved to the Fox.

Violet, mother of five, has always been popular with her faithful regulars—but the Fox is on the road to nowhere and has little passing trade. There is no local industry within striking distance, and Meesden itself is a quiet place with no activities like village cricket to provide a spin-off for the local.

"It is just not a viable living," said Violet. "Many weekday lunch times go by without a single customer. I shall be sorry to go. I have enjoyed it and shall miss it very much."

But her motherly face will not disappear completely from the local bar scene as she plans to offer her services to local licensees to fill in to give them nights off and holidays.

She is a popular personality among local publicans. She is a committee member and keen fund-raiser for the Hertford Ladies' Auxiliary, which she joined 14 years ago, and she will continue as an honorary member. Her colleagues in the branch presented her with a handbag as a goodbye present.

Tom and their son Douglas are both keen bar billiards players—a game which used to be very popular at the pub— and Tom holds the Buntingford League landlords' cup, having won it for the last three years before the league folded up in 1978–79.

The Prossers and their unmarried son are moving to Willow Close, Great Hormead.

There was a farewell party last Saturday for some of their old customers from Enfield. But there will be one or two more gatherings for the locals before they finally shut the door of the Fox for the last time.

Figure 1.4   An article in the Hertfordshire Mercury

of individuals and figure 1.1 in the chapter gives a further example of the problems caused by immobility in rural areas. A number of projects suggest themselves: fieldwork could be undertaken to record and map service provision within a sub-district of East Hertfordshire and compare it with the recent past (see chapter 2 in this book on data sources); daily and weekly 'action spaces' of the rural dwellers could be mapped and compared with those of a sample of nearby urban dwellers; or a study could be attempted with the aim of determining which groups (women or men, the young or the old etc.) suffer most from the lack of public transport, social amenities and shops.

In the first of the above suggestions, fieldwork will be combined with a close examination of secondary, documentary sources of information, but in all three suggestions the aim is to find out how people behave in terms of their shopping habits, journeys to school, college or work and their leisure activities. The questionnaire would seem to be appropriate, therefore, as the main fieldwork tool.

Perhaps the greatest practical problem facing the student in any of these projects is the question of his or her own personal mobility as the study will involve visiting several, maybe quite isolated, village communities. The determined student will overcome this, perhaps with the aid of a bicycle, but the fact remains that the size of the study area would have to be carefully limited (the whole of the rural district of East Hertfordshire would surely be out of the question).

1.6   Working towards a concrete goal

The aim of this section is to draw together some of the thoughts introduced in the previous pages. Again, it must be emphasised that a recipe for guaranteed success in practical geography cannot be written owing to the diversity of the subject-matter and the methods available for use; each project will have its own unique problems. What can be set out, though, are guidelines that can help the student avoid the common pitfalls to be found at all stages of the project's execution.

The most obvious and damaging pitfall is to be unclear about the precise goals of the project. Fieldwork, which includes the accurate observation and recording of information is a fundamental skill of the investigator, but it is not an end in itself. Unless the investigator is absolutely clear as to the purpose of the fieldwork, he or she will be left with a mass of inadequately *used* information; that is, it will be only half-digested and not analysed sufficiently to enable the researcher to make sound conclusions. Whatever the origin of the initial idea to be investigated, therefore, the student must spend time reading, discussing and even making a reconnoitre visit to the study area. Before work begins in earnest he or she should be able to state in just a few short sentences what it is he or she hopes to achieve. If this can be done, then the energy of the investigator can be single-mindedly channelled into the task of achieving the stated objectives. Without this kind of discipline the project can take the form of a mish-mash of loosely connected pieces of information. The researcher is not in *control* of the data; it is rather the other way round, the data controlling the researcher!

This is one good reason why the hypothesis-testing approach to field investigation is useful and often productive. Figure 1.5 shows a simple flow diagram to illustrate this approach. In effect, the problem to be investigated is narrowed down to one hypothesis (although some studies may propose two or even three). An hypothesis is a statement or proposition that can be tested for its validity. If, after the fieldwork and analysis of data, the hypothesis is seen to be wrong then it can be rejected and a modified or even a completely new hypothesis put in its place. Sometimes the hypothesis can be accepted as being very probably a sound statement. In either case, the fieldwork comes to a clear and definite conclusion and, so long as the initial hypothesis was sensible and the data collection and analysis accurate, then the project should be worthwhile. In order to confirm to yourself that you comprehend this properly, refer back to section 1.2 and state the hypothesis that you would test in a study of 'Brennan's Law' in your local urban area.

As you may have found in other texts on hypothesis testing in geography, it is normal to transform your hypothesis into the *null hypothesis* before testing. The null hypothesis (Ho) is the hypothesis that assumes nothing about a particular relationship or geographical pattern. If Ho can be rejected, perhaps using some form of statistical testing procedure, then there is a high probability that your initial hypothesis is acceptable. In the case of the Brennan's Law project, Ho might be stated as follows: 'Shoppers in town X have no preference for stores in the direction of the town centre as compared with stores located away from the town centre.' If your fieldwork enables you to reject this null hypothesis then the implication is that shoppers do have a preference for stores in the direction of the town centre, and Brennan's Law is supported.

It will have occurred to the reader that not all projects can be reduced to the hypothesis testing approach and in some ways this procedure is constricting. Nonetheless, most projects can be narrowed down to a short list of aims, and it would be good practice to attempt to do this for the ideas outlined in sections 1.3, 1.4 and 1.5. In these projects, the investigator should be in the position of knowing the kind of results that are being sought, although with-

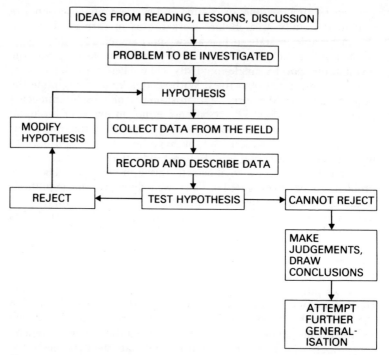

Figure 1.5   The 'Hypothesis Testing' approach to fieldwork studies

> *This approach usually involves statistical testing methods, but it need not; cartographic analysis can be used, for example. Its main strength is that if forces you to work to a very well-defined goal; by merely completing the project, you are almost forced to come to some kind of conclusion.*

out a definite picture of the precise nature of the outcome.

Once concrete goals are established the investigator must then clarify the various stages of the project work:

1. Where to find and how to obtain relevant information.
2. What techniques to employ to record the information.
3. How to analyse the data.
4. What conclusions can be drawn.
5. How to present the completed work.

2
Preliminary sources and some preliminary ideas

2.1 Background reading

In the previous chapter we outlined, through the use of examples, the scope of local studies projects in human geography. Before making a final decision about a topic there are perhaps two fundamental questions that the student ought to ask him or herself:

1. Is this topic geographical?
2. Do I understand fully the implications of this topic?

The first question may seem somewhat strange; surely if one is studying geography a selected topic for local investigation will, by definition, be geographical! However, the situation is sometimes not so clear cut. For example, a study of nineteenth-century public health conditions in a nearby town could be a very sound historical –geographical investigation, mapping the incidence of disease or the spread of public health improvements such as a piped sewage system. But it could also degenerate into a straight historical account of conditions in the nineteenth-century town with little or no *geographical* perspective. To be geographical means that the project would normally include some sort of *spatial* component. Thus, a geographical study would often investigate a *pattern*, or the *distribution* of some kind of human phenomenon, or the influence of something (a factory or a shopping centre) on the *space* around. To explain the pattern, the geography would often have to seek non-spatial processes but this does not detract from the spatial, or geographical, problem under scrutiny.

The second of the above questions will be more obvious to the student. It is clearly not wise to embark upon a project unless the topic to be investigated is clearly understood. For example in section 1.5, 'action spaces' were introduced as an aspect of a study on rural problems worth investigation. But, if the concept of an individual's action space is only partially understood, the fieldwork instigated to measure action spaces stands a good chance of being imperfect or even inadequate.

Consequently, it is a vital prerequisite of successful local investigations that BACKGROUND READING is undertaken before the final title is decided upon and certainly before any hypothesis is formulated. After all, the student should aim to become something of a mini-expert on the particular field of enquiry being attempted.

Reading can be divided into three broad areas and can be completed in the following logical order:

1. Wide reading around the subject. This is done from standard text books that are easily available from your department, school or college.

2. Books and articles of a more specialised nature can suggest themselves from your initial reading, or can be suggested by your teacher or tutor.

3. Books and articles specifically on the *techniques* of field investigation and data analysis should be consulted in order that you prepare yourself properly. Books such as the *'Science in Geography'* *Series* (Books 1–4, B. P. FitzGerald (ed.), OUP 1974) are very useful in this respect, as is the *'Geography Applied'* *Series* which includes one volume each on 'Urban Development and Planning' and 'Manufacturing Industry' (J. Hancock (ed.), Basil Blackwell 1980). Also helpful on specific techniques are articles in magazines such as *'Geo'* (Elizabeth Weaver Ltd.) and *'Teaching Geography'* (The Geographical Association), both of which your teacher can put you in touch with if need be.

2.2   Secondary sources for local investigation

Once the problem under investigation has been decided upon (see again figure 1.1) the manner in which it should be approached has to be determined, and potential data sources have to be investigated. One huge data source is, of course, 'the field', but much information need not be collected first hand. Much is available in documentary form and, if so, should be used; it is clearly a waste of time and energy to collect information yourself when it already exists as a 'secondary source'. It is the purpose of this section to briefly review what secondary sources are available and, in section 2.3, to give some hints as to some of the potential problems that exist for the unwary researcher.

First, we should attempt to define what we mean by secondary source. A sharp definition is not easy to give, but there is a distinction between secondary information and primary information. The latter implies information collected specifically for a defined purpose and, therefore, includes all direct field observation and data collection. The former includes information that has been assembled by other agencies and not necessarily for any specific purpose. As a general rule, the potential of secondary sources for your project should be investigated prior to engaging yourself in time consuming, and sometimes costly, fieldwork.

There are, of course, literally thousands of potential sources of secondary information. The vast majority of these, however, are unusable in the context of practical *local* geography owing to the scale differential between the project and the source. You may well have come across the *'Geographical Digest'* published by Philips every year which is a veritable mine of information – but all on a scale unsuitable for a local investigation. The same can be said of other sources such as *UK Facts* (Rose and McAllister, Macmillan, 1982), or the *Family Expenditure Survey* (HMSO). *Regional Trends*, covering many aspects of social and economic activity, also does not present statistics on a fine enough scale. All these sources contain valuable material for the geographer, but, in the context of local investigation, not more than the barest background information can be supplied by them.

Thus we can narrow down our discussion to just a few very useful secondary sources:

the 'everyday sources'
the Census of Population
Local Authority documentation
archive sources
other sources.

'EVERYDAY SOURCES'

What we have called 'everyday sources' include documents that you may not have even realised are data sources. The *Yellow Pages* in the telephone directory is an invaluable listing of industrial and commercial operations in the area, and their addresses. The *Ordnance Survey* maps, especially at the larger scales of 1 : 25000 or even 1 : 10000 are obviously useful for recording data in the field, but can also be used in their own right as an historical source, if, for example, the physical growth of a settlement is an issue under investigation. A little more enquiry at the local library may well reveal other sources of this type such as *'Kelly's Directory'*, back copies of which can be used as an historical source of information on the commercial functions of settlements. Libraries will also have Trade Directories containing up-to-date information of the same type.

CENSUS OF POPULATION

The Census of Population is of great potential use for a wide range of project topics. It was begun in 1801 and has been taken every ten years since then (except for the war year of 1941). It provides figures of a very general type in the Preliminary Report tables and

County Monitors but also data relating to the smallest spatial unit officially recognised, the ward. It is quite likely that a local geography investigation would cover an area that contains several wards and, thus, these data are of great value; indeed professional geographers and planners rely on this information, contained in the Ward and Parish Monitors and the small area statistics to a very large degree in their research.

Without doubt, the best way to really appreciate the possibilities of the Census reports is for the student to go to the local *library* and dedicate an hour or two getting to know them. At first, they might appear confusing and difficult to cope with and trying to compare the Census tables for different years, for example, can be difficult because local authority boundaries, for which Census figures are given, have changed several times.

What follows below is a background perspective of what the Census aims to do and the type of questions that appear on the form issued to households to complete every ten years. Both the precise aims and the form the questions take vary slightly between census dates, of course, and the 1981 Census is used as an example. First of all, there follows an extract from the instructions given to each household in England in March 1981:

> 'A household comprises *either* one person living alone *or* a group of persons (who may or may not be related) living at the same address with common housekeeping. Persons staying temporarily with the household are included.'

> To the Head or Joint Heads or members of the Household:
> Please complete this census form and have it ready to be collected by the census enumerator for your area. He or she will call for the form on Monday 8 April 1981 or soon after . . . .
> Your replies will be treated in STRICT CONFIDENCE. They will be used to produce statistics but your name and address will NOT be fed into the census computer.
> After the census, the forms will be locked away for 100 years before they are passed to the Public Record Office . . ..

The form consists of a number of questions (sixteen), the majority of which are 'closed', as opposed to 'open', meaning that they resemble multiple choice questions where all possible responses are given and the respondent must choose one. The questions are concerned with housing, work, transport and the characteristics of the members of the household. By way of illustration, in tables 2.1 and 2.2 we present just two of the 1981 Census questions which may be considered particularly interesting to the geography student.

Table 2.1   1981 Census question on household amenities

Amenities

Has your household the use of the following amenities on these premises?
(Please tick the appropriate boxes.)

A fixed bath or shower permanently connected to a water supply and a waste pipe
1. ☐ YES – for use only by this household
2. ☐ YES – for use also by another household
3. ☐ No fixed bath or shower

A flush toilet (WC) with entrance inside the building
1. ☐ YES – for use only by this household
2. ☐ YES – for use also by another household
3. ☐ No inside flush toilet (WC)

A flush toilet (WC) with entrance outside the building
1. ☐ YES – for use only by this household
2. ☐ YES – for use also by another household
3. ☐ No outside flush toilet (WC)

Table 2.2   1981 Census question on journey to work

Daily journey to work

Please tick the appropriate box to show how the longest part, by distance, of the person's daily journey to work is normally made.

For a person using different means of transport on different days show the means most often used.

Car or van includes three-wheeled cars and motor caravans.

1. ☐ British Rail train.
2. ☐ Underground, tube, metro etc.
3. ☐ Bus, minibus or coach (public or private)
4. ☐ Motor cycle, scooter, moped
5. ☐ Car or van – pool, sharing driving
6. ☐ Car or van – driver
7. ☐ Car or van – passenger
8. ☐ Pedal cycle
9. ☐ On foot
10. ☐ Other (please specify) ....
11. ☐ Works mainly at home

Source: Office of Population Censuses and Surveys

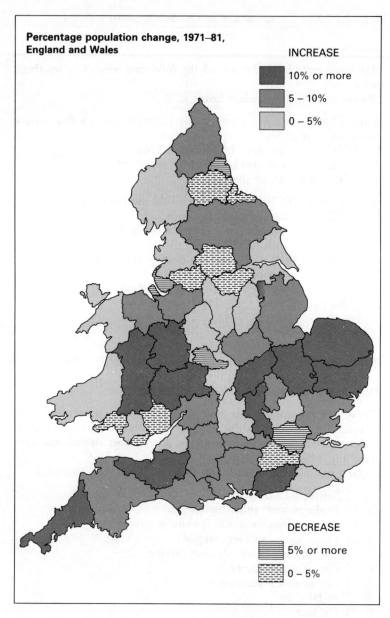

Figure 2.1   A Guardian *report on initial findings from the 1981 Census*

The map and the text contains interesting information for the student of Geography, with implications for studies of both urban and rural areas.

CENSUS SHOWS DRIFT OUT OF TOWNS

Population growth in England and Wales over the last 10 years was minimal, Gareth Parry reports

THE move back to the country continues, according to provisional results from the 1981 census, which indicates an overall population increase in England and Wales of some 260,000 to a total of 49 million.

The half per cent growth over the last decade is within 0.2 per cent of the number which had been expected. But the report shows that population growth in the 1970s was very much less than the 5 per cent in each of the previous two decades.

Each of the three regions without a major industrial conurbation showed substantial population gains: the South-west was up 246,000; East Anglia, 196,000; and the East Midlands, 174,000.

London had one of the biggest loss rates — its population is now below seven million for the first time since 1901.

But the population shift in the South-east is probably the most interesting of all the regions, showing the most dramatic reversal in trends compared with 10 years previously. It has changed from a growth region to one which has lost the largest number of people; and it contains the two extremes — Milton Keynes, with its 85 per cent increase, and Kensington and Chelsea, with its 26 per cent decrease.

The 1981 Census Preliminary Report: England and Wales, published today, shows that the population of England increased by 203,000 (0.4 per cent) in 10 years while that of Wales rose by 59,000 (2.2 per cent). Scotland's population fell by 112,000 (2.1 per cent).

The preliminary report gives the first results from the census taken on April 5 and, although the figures are still provisional, they are published at this early stage because they provide important new evidence about population in certain areas. These provisional figures will be replaced by final corrected figures in the detailed county reports and county monitors which it is planned to publish from November onwards.

If all goes well, the main priority tables for all the counties will be available by May, 1982, in time for block grant calculation for 1983–4.

Four regions of England showed substantial population losses. The largest in terms of numbers were for the North-west and South-east, which each lost about 200,000. In terms of percentages, the North-west experienced the greatest decline (2.9 per cent) followed by the North (1.4 per cent).

In the South-east, a loss of 756,000 in Greater London was only partly offset by growth in the rest of the region to give 1.2 per cent decline overall. London's population fell by 10 per cent to below seven million for the first time since the 1901 census.

Differences in net levels of migration into or out of the regions are given as the main reason for the regional variations in population change.

The preliminary report gives provisional totals for people present on census night for 370 districts of England and Wales and for the 33 London boroughs. The preliminary report for a few local authority areas give a misleading indication of change because the 1981 census was taken two weeks before Easter at a time when most educational institutions were on vacation, while the 1971 census was taken two weeks after Easter, in term time.

Generally, the population of large cities and conurbations fell — the larger the city, the greater the fall — while the population of the urban fringes and the more rural areas grew.

Inner London lost half a million people, about 18 per cent of its population. Manchester, Liverpool, and Birmingham each lost between 90,000 and 100,000 people — 17, 16, and 8 per cent respectively, Newcastle upon Tyne lost 10 per cent, Sheffield 6 per cent, and Leeds 5 per cent.

Most districts which are not dominated by a large or medium-sized city grew in population, though often by less than in the previous decade.

An important change, compared with the 1971 census, has been the marked decline in the number of rapidly growing districts. The 1981 census showed only 41 districts whose population had increased by over 15 per cent since the preceding census; in 1971 there were 140 such districts — over three times as many.

1981 Census Preliminary Report; England and Wales. Stationery Office £4.80 net.

Questions concerning the characteristics of individuals include items on place of birth, type of employment, qualifications obtained after school, marital status, etc. The housing questions also include type of *tenure* and number of rooms, and the work section includes a question on the place of work. It can be seen that the census, when completed, throws up an enormous amount of information and even with the assistance of computers it takes about three years to complete the publication programme. The Preliminary Report Tables are the first to emerge and the results of this initial analysis are usually widely reported in the press revealing important population shifts, for example, as in figure 2.1

1   One vital task for the people charged with the job of designing and preparing census forms is to make the instructions as clear and as unambiguous as possible. Examine again the extract from the instructions to households and tables 2.1 and 2.2. Give two or three examples of how the wording or the layout has been specifically designed to avoid ambiguity.

2. Imagine that you are interested in attempting a local studies project to investigate how aspects of the social-geographical characteristics of an area have changed in recent years.
   (*a*) In what way might the information in figure 2.1 be of help, if any?
   (*b*) List the various features of the local geography that would be worth investigation, for which information might already be published in the form of census records in your library.
   (*c*) Can you indentify potentially interesting features of the locality for which information would not be forthcoming from the census?

Discussion

A most skilful task that the designer of instructions or questions must undertake is to predict any problems that may arise over the understanding or misunderstanding of the terminology used. It is essential that everyone who is asked the question has the same understanding of the question. The designer must ensure, therefore, that definitions are clear and that all 'grey areas' are interpreted in the same manner. With reference to the former, ask yourself whether, having read the definition on page 24, you are clear as to what is meant by the term 'household'. With reference to the latter, note how, in table 2.2, the designer of the question has predicted a number of possible grey areas – for example, the person who travels to work using various modes of transport from day to day – and has attempted to standardise the responses by way of clear instructions.

Without studying the census tables for a while beforehand, it is very difficult to imagine their full potential. The Preliminary Report tables can be utilised in the sense that they can help 'set the scene' by giving general background information; the fact that your local area may have been experiencing an influx of population and has this characteristic in common with a number of other areas of a similar type of location, might make a worthwhile introductory point. At a ward level you will find detailed information on population, housing, status and work characteristics, all of which may prove useful in the main body of your investigation. What the census will not tell you, however, is precise information for *spatial units defined by yourself*; for example, you might wish to compare social-geographical characteristics amongst a number of housing estates in your town, in which case your own survey may have to be undertaken. The Census does give information on car ownership per household but it does not give details on other aspects of material well-being such as the number of households owning a freezer or a video. Of course, more esoteric, but nevertheless potentially interesting, information is not supplied by the Census – such as households growing their own vegetables or renting an allotment. Again, this would necessitate your own specially designed survey and this is discussed more fully in chapter 3.

LOCAL AUTHORITIES
Local Authorities collect and store a great deal of information, much of which is open to public scrutiny and potentially useful to the local investigator. Some authorities are, indeed, very helpful to the student providing staff who have, as part of their responsibilities, the specific task to satisfy public enquiries and even making space available for the student to work. All local authorities are approachable, however, and most will offer help if approached in the right manner. For example, a letter or a telephone call briefly introducing yourself and outlining what information you need is a good idea before you visit the authorities offices in person; you might even ask for an appointment at a time convenient to them. Also, it invariably pays off for the student to know *what* information he or she requires; there is nothing more perplexing to the local authority official than being asked vague and ill-thought-out questions about information that the student is not too sure about, because it often seems to the official that the student is really asking the local authority to do the 'spade work'.

A particularly accessible source of data is the record of *rateable values*, and these figures can be of use in a number of projects ranging from CBD studies of towns to housing studies. The rateable value represents the local authority's assessment of the value of a property for the purpose of collecting local authority revenue through the rates system. The rateable value varies according to the size and amenities of the property, and also the location of the property and it is the latter which makes it an interesting figure from the geographical point of view. When using this information it is, of course, vital to remember to standardise the figures copied from the local authority's records especially in central area studies where the sizes of shops vary enormously making 'raw' rateable values hard to compare. The standard technique used in this context is the calculation of the 'foot-frontage value' (the rateable value of the shop divided by its frontage, measured in feet, onto the pavement – the frontage being an easily obtained measure of the shop's size).

Local authorities are responsible for policy and planning in the local framework. The specific responsibility depends on the type of local authority and table 2.3 summarises this. Plans and policies for all aspects of local administration are published from time to time and such documents can be helpful to the local geographical investigation as they often contain useable information in the form of maps and tables. Sometimes local plans will even present the results of specially commissioned surveys of residents on matters ranging from shopping behaviour to opinions on a controversial local development like the building of a bypass or the redevelopment of a shopping street.

*Table 2.3   Responsibilities of different Local Government units (England and Wales only).**

	Planning	Education	Environmental Health	Housing	Recreation	Traffic
County	✓	✓			✓	✓
Districts	✓		✓	✓	✓	
Metropolitan County	✓				✓	✓
Metropolitan Districts	✓	✓	✓	✓	✓	
GLC	✓			✓	✓	✓
London Boroughs	✓	✓	✓	✓	✓	

*Note: this is a generalised list, and individual responsibilities under any heading may show slight differences.

The *County Structure Plan* is, perhaps, the most important document of this type but in some ways the least useful in a direct and practical sense. Once again, scale is the problem as the Structure Plan concerns the whole county whereas your study will have a much, much narrower brief. Nevertheless, it can serve a useful purpose in putting your study into a proper context. The Plan describes the existing patterns of population, housing conditions, industry, the transport network and shopping provision – just to mention a few of the sub-sections contained within it. Below is an extract from the Hertfordshire Structure Plan, a section that concerns shopping provision in the county:

The Hertfordshire Shopping '*Hierarchy*'
A classification of the relative status of shopping centres has been obtained primarily from a study of the range of facilities available, taking into account figures of turnover and floorspace, the constraints imposed on shopping expansion by conservation and environmental considerations and known proposals for increases in floorspace and improvements to car parking and servicing arrangements in each centre. The hierarchy is set out below:

1. *Sub-regional centres.* These are the higher level centres which provide a basic framework for shopping activity in the County. A full range of goods and services will generally be found in each centre with a large proportion of floorspace and above three quarters of turnover in durable goods. The 'major' centres act as a local alternative to central London, whilst the 'minor' centres are smaller in scale.

    Major sub-regional: Stevenage
    Watford
    Minor sub-regional: Hemel Hempstead
    Hitchin
    St Albans
    Welwyn Garden City

2. *District centres.* These centres are limited in range of goods and types of shops provided and consequently perform a more local function than the sub-regional centres. The absence of several important types of shops will mean that some local trade will tend to be lost to higher level centres.

    Major districts: Bishop's Stortford
    Hatfield
    Hertford
    Hoddesdon
    Letchworth
    Waltham Cross
    Minor districts: Berkhamsted
    Borehamwood

Harpenden
Potters Bar
Rickmansworth
Royston
Ware

Local districts: Baldock
Bushey
Cheshunt
Chorley Wood
North Watford
Radlett
Sawbridgeworth
South Oxhey
Tring

(*Source*: Hertfordshire County Structure Plan pp. 61–2)

The County *policy* towards shopping is then explained in detail, but is also stated in essence in the following words:

> The County Council will continue to consider all proposals for additional shopping development in the light of the established shopping hierarchy and will pursue a policy on the basis of all needs being met within existing central areas and local centres.

1. The description of the existing pattern is clearly written in the context or framework of Central Place Theory (see book 3, *Urban Systems*, chapters 3 and 4). Remind yourself of the underlying concepts highlighted by CPT; how does the County Plan distinguish the two main levels of the hierarchy of central places in Hertfordshire?

2. Is the hierarchy likely to change much during the forseeable future?

3. Briefly outline one local investigation that may suggest itself to you from the extract.

Discussion

The County Plan recognises that shopping centres can be distinguished on two counts: first, on account of their size which determines the purchasing power of the settlement which in turn influences the type and number of retail outlets the town can support, secondly, by the power of attraction of the shopping centres (the sub-regional centres winning some of the trade of the district centres as a result of their ability to offer a wider selection of shops including the more specialised shops). These ideas relate to the concept of the *Threshold* and the *Range* respectively, both of which arise out of Central Place Theory. Even though no precise data are given in the extract, it is interesting to note that the sub-regional centres are defined as having at least three quarters of their turnover in 'durable goods' (furniture, electrical goods, and so on). It is also relevant to note that this is the kind of information (i.e. the turnover of shops and stores) that the student is most unlikely to obtain directly him or herself, as individual store managers or shopowners are not willing to divulge 'sensitive' information of this sort. The hierarchy set out in the Structure Plan is not likely to change substantially in the coming years as the policy is clearly conservative and does not envisage that the shopping needs of the population will necessitate any major departure from the present pattern.

This is not to say, however, that minor shifts or changes have not occurred in the local area, possibly as a result of developments in the local infrastructure – say the building of a large car park in a *local* shopping centre attracting shoppers away from the nearby *district* centre. Attempting to measure such small-scale aspects of shopping behaviour could form the basis of local projects. Furthermore, the Structure Plan makes some general comments about the sphere of influence of, say, the sub-regional centres; however, it is not able to give specific details about the shopping habits of specific localities; a field exercise to establish the spheres of influence, or trade areas, of 'Neighbourhood', 'Local' and 'District' shopping centres in your locality might be very rewarding. The Structure Plan can provide a firm framework for such a study, but more precise data will have to be sought elsewhere, or from fieldwork.

ARCHIVE SOURCES
Archive sources are various and take many forms. For the purpose of this discussion they are distinguished from Census Reports and from Local Authority documentation in that they are histori-cal and usually in the written form (as opposed to being mainly contemporary and primarily statistical in nature). The main sources of archive material are the library service and, once again, the Local Authority. A local study using archive material would prob-ably be an historical-geographical investigation and is very likely to depend almost wholly on secondary sources; it would prob-ably be necessary, therefore, to make special arrangements with the library or County Archive office so that the student can spend some considerable time at work. (You will not be able to take such material home with you!) It is not possible to give an exhaustive list of such material here, but the type of material that would be interesting could be *Medical Officer of Health* reports which had to be written in the latter half of the nineteenth century and form a

useful, if disjointed, source of information on health and social conditions in the Victorian town, for example. The results of some historial-geographical research are described in book 4, *The City*, chapter 2.

OTHER SOURCES

There are other sources of secondary information and the perceptive and alert student will find them. One potential source not mentioned yet is the *computer file*. All schools now have computer facilities and many have well-established links with outside agencies. Through either the school's resources, or the school in conjunction with external help, it is increasingly possible to tap very promising sources of data. One example, (which could be used effectively in connection with the Central Place example discussed above), is 'Herts '71' which is a data file containing precise information about all settlements in Hertfordshire listing all shops and services existing in settlements in 1971. This information would, of course, provide a suitable basis for a study of changing service provision in the local area over the last 15 years or so. Your school or college should be able to put you in touch with such a source of data, and give the technical assistance in order to extract the information you desire.

2.3 The potential and the limitations of secondary sources

It has already been mentioned in this chapter that the aim here is not to attempt to write an exhaustive list of secondary sources. Even if this could be done with confidence, it would quickly become out of date and therefore misleading because new material is constantly being published. We have mentioned, and in some cases discussed, the widely accessible and usable sources such as the Census, but, in the end, it is the determination of the student that will decide on whether sources are unearthed and what use is made of them. Following the simple guidelines outlined in the previous section will stand the student in good stead; for example, if up-to-date unemployment and job vacancy statistics are required for a project then a polite letter including more than just vague requests will almost certainly meet with a positive response from the local Jobcentre – and if they cannot help, they will advise you of who can.

It is the manner in which the student approaches secondary sources that is the vital issue, and perhaps the following 'check-list' of questions will help the student maximise the utility derived from them:

1. Have I exhausted the *school's resources* of text books (for background reading), articles (for background reading and on specific techniques I may require), and other sources (planning documents, computer stored data)?

2. Have I made contact with *outside agencies*: local libraries, local authorities, the rates office, Jobcentre, university, polytechnic or college etc?

3. Did I achieve what I set out to achieve in 1 and 2 above? If not, why not? Do I need to plan further reading or additional visits?

4. Have I been thoughtful and discriminatory concerning the secondary information I have chosen to use? Are the data I have extracted of direct relevance to my selected area of investigation?

5. Have I kept an accurate list of all the books, articles and other secondary sources that I have used? Apart from being useful to have in case you need to refer back to a source of some description, you will need this information for the bibliography, or list of references, at the end of your work.

Perhaps the greatest problem concerning secondary data is the question of scale and, as this is a question of wide implications in geographical investigation, we shall deal with it separately in the following section.

2.4 The scale problem

The information that a student might extract from a secondary source is built up from many individual observations. The records of each individual are not published, of course, and the hundreds or thousands of individual characteristics are usually aggregated for specified spatial units. These statistics – ratios or aggregated totals – become the data that the student then must work with. Figure 2.2 shows the arrangements of spatial units within London. It is a hierarchical arrangement, a structure of space which is broken down into successive levels of smaller areas. Figure 2.3 shows a similar, if more detailed, arrangement for the 1971 Census of Great Britain. A massive problem to the investigator is that the units at any level in the hierarchy can vary in both shape and size. In addition, the boundaries of the units are not drawn with geographical research in mind and often follow old-established local government boundaries.

As D. M. Smith (1977, pp. 30–33) writes:

A major shortcoming of administrative areas as units of observation is that they vary considerably in size and shape. The counties,

(a) Borough population density, 1971

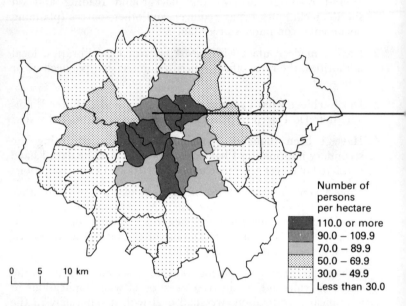

Number of
persons
per hectare

	110.0 or more
	90.0 – 109.9
	70.0 – 89.9
	50.0 – 69.9
	30.0 – 49.9
	Less than 30.0

0   5   10 km

(d) Population density of enumeration districts in St John's Ward, Camden, 1971

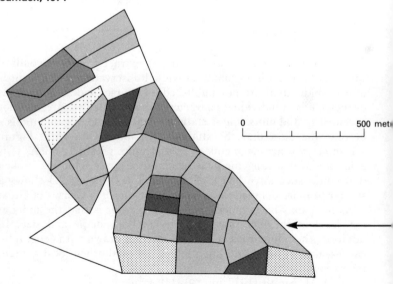

0   500 met

Figure 2.2   The hierarchical structure of areal sub-divisions in London for the 1971 Census (from Shepherd et al., 1975)

(b) Population density of wards in Camden, 1971

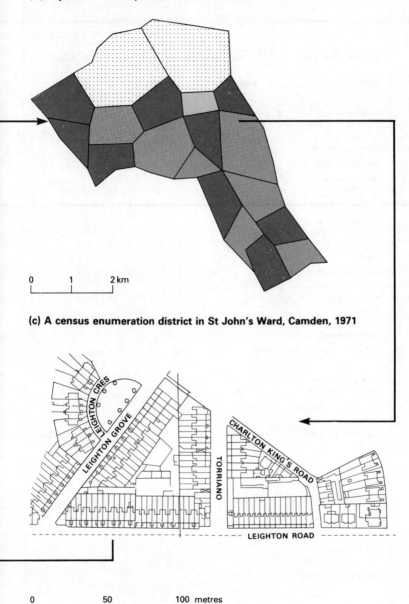

0   1   2 km

(c) A census enumeration district in St John's Ward, Camden, 1971

0   50   100 metres

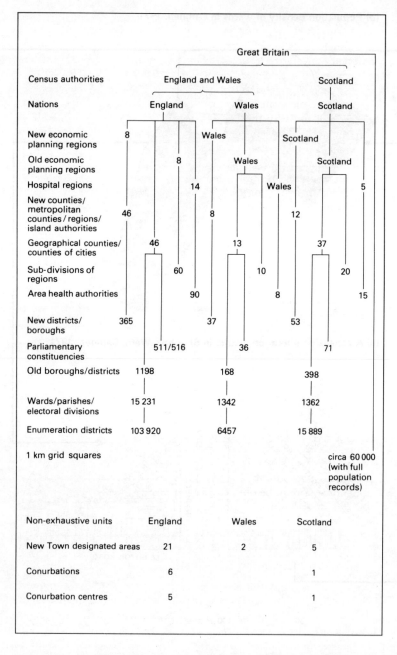

Figure 2.3   Reporting units for the 1971 Census (Office of Population Censuses and Surveys)

parishes and other civil divisions of Britain are an obvious case in point. In the United States, the western states and counties are much larger than in New England, and American counties can vary in shape from perfectly square in northern Texas to extremely long and narrow in parts of the Appalachians. This affects geographical description, for a large area may have a large occurrence of some condition simply because of its size or because of the way the boundary is drawn. A group of small or narrow areas may give an exaggerated impression of inter-area movement (e.g. journey to work patterns) simply because so many boundaries are crossed. There are also technical problems in the analysis of numerical data compiled for geographical areas, for measures of areal distribution are sensitive to the size of the units of observation and can give different results at different levels of aggregation.

Few of the systems of areal classifications used for compiling official figures on social or economic affairs have been designed specifically for this purpose. Generally they follow some established system used for the organisation of local government. Such areas may have no social or economic significance, and their boundaries may have been laid down well before human activity assumed its present spatial form. Sensible definitions of relevant study areas can thus be difficult if official data sources have to be used. One way out of this problem is for the investigator to collect his own information, and aggregate individual observations according to whatever areal classifications seems most appropriate, though this can be extremely laborious and time consuming.

1. Smith's comments include an example of how small areal units may give a misleading impression of journey to work patterns. He then goes on to suggest that the distribution patterns of phenomena may be open to misleading interpretation as a result of the spatial units of the aggregated data. Examine figure 2.4 and attempt to describe for yourself how the description of the point pattern shown will vary wildly depending on whether the whole pattern is taken as one unit, or whether just the north–east or south–west quadrants are chosen.

2. One way around the 'scale problem' is for the investigator to adopt his or her own survey within boundaries defined by him or herself. For large-scale research projects the cost of this might be prohibitive. Therefore, can you suggest how official data collection could ease the problem for the researcher? (It will be worth studying figure 2.3 carefully, as the 1971 Census went some way to ease the problem.)

Discussion

Figure 2.4 shows a point pattern which, if taken as a whole, shows a tendency to cluster along the NE–SW axis of the area, the NW and SE quadrants being underrepresented in so far as this particular distribution is concerned. However, if the NE quadrant alone is examined one can see a remarkably regular pattern. In the SW, on the other hand, the pattern is quite random. In other words, the spatial unit chosen for the basis of study effects how the pattern can be interpreted. It is far more than just a philosophical problem and in some cases how a pattern is described or where a boundary line on a map is drawn might be a serious issue for the local investigator.

Unless the individual results of a census are stored in a huge data store in a computer, so that a researcher can extract precisely the data he or she wants for areas he or she has defined, then the best compromise is for the Census officials to aggregate the data into the smallest convenient areal units. The former is certainly contro-

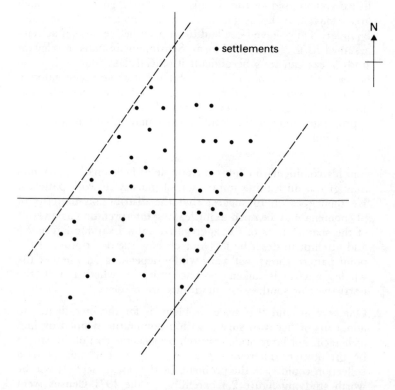

Figure 2.4   Pattern variation with scale (after Chisholm, 1975)

versial because the individual may feel that confidentiality would
not be able to be guaranteed, and it is interesting that the 1971
Census of Great Britain compiled statistics for hundred metre
squares based upon the national grid. This enables the investigator
to carefully assemble grid squares of data to approximate any larger
area he or she wishes to consider.

The problem of scale can be examined in another way. So far,
we have discussed the way in which the scale of analysis may affect
our interpretation of a *pattern*, but it may also affect the validity of
our explanations and inferences. This is summarised succinctly in
the following passage from Short's invaluable book for the urban
geographer, *Urban Data Sources* in a section entitled 'Scale and the
ecological fallacy' (1975, p. 24):

> It is important to ensure that the scale of analysis, and the data,
> are appropriate to the hypotheses under consideration. Many of
> the hypotheses which we seek to test in urban geography are
> concerned with the relationships between characteristics of *indi-*
> *viduals*, either persons or households. Unfortunately most of the
> official data sources, especially the Census, provide information
> not on individuals, but for *groups* of individuals in specific areas
> of the city. For example, if we wish to test the hypothesis that
> persons in private renting are younger than those in owner-
> occupation (think of the reasons why this should or should not
> be true), we need data on the mode of tenure of individuals of
> different ages. However, from the Census we can only obtain
> information on the proportion of persons in different tenure
> categories and the proportion of persons of different ages. If for
> 10 areas in a city we have a pattern as depicted in figure 2.5, then
> we can only *suggest* that there is a relationship between the age
> and tenure of individuals. The data do not prove it, since it may

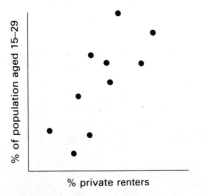

Figure 2.5   Hypothetical relationship between tenure and age

be that the person aged 15–29 years may not necessarily be in private renting. To make conclusions at the individual scale from analysis of data at the aggregate scale, in this case to make conclusions at the individual level from the analysis of data referring to population in ten areas, is to make the 'ecological fallacy'.

Another way of saying 'to make the "ecological fallacy" ' would be 'jumping to false conclusions' and of course the local investigator must always be wary of falling into this particular trap.

Thus, secondary sources of information offer both promise and potential traps for the unwary and, to echo Smith's final comment, direct field observation (in conditions controlled by the investigator) may be best – if not the only – source of data for your local studies project. It is to this that our discussion now turns.

3
Out into the field . . .

3.1 Preparing yourself

We have seen that, useful though secondary sources can be, documented records, including the Census, are very often inadequate for our precise needs. Often, then, we must go out into 'the field' – the neighbourhood, the CBD, the town or wherever – and gather our own information. As we have emphasied on a number of occasions it is essential that the student is properly prepared *before* embarking on the fieldwork and the purpose of this section is to outline what this entails in more detail. Certainly, there is more involved than ensuring that you have waterproof clothing, the necessary paper and pencils and warm footwear! The following passage from David Smith's book *Patterns in Human Geography* (p. 15) will set the scene.

Human beings arrange their lives in geographical space. They exist and perform their activities at specific locations, and they move or distribute things in certain directions. They thus give character to places or areas, differentiating and connecting them with respect to various aspects of the human condition. The geographical expression of man's existence can be thought of very simply as a geometry of points, lines and areas. Production locations, places of residence, settlements and so on form patterns of points or *nodes* around which life is organised. Lines of communication and transportation form *networks* of movements and interaction. Human differentiation of geographical space forms systems of *regions*, or areas distinguished by some particular characteristics bestowing homogeneity or functional cohesion. The man-made landscape is a collage of these nodes, networks and regions.

The analysis of this geometry of spatial form is the basic task of human geography. But before the existing situation can be explained, or improved upon, it has to be accurately described. This implies a careful process of observation in which the results can preferably be expressed in numerical form for the precise description of human geographical patterns is basic to their eventual understanding.

1. What three elements of the 'geometry of spatial form' does Smith identify? Very briefly, describe a project topic in which two, or if possible all three, of these geographical elements are important features.

2. Are Smith's elements all inclusive, or can you think of other spatial forms that could become the focus of a geographical inquiry?

3. Is it in any way useful to divide geographical analysis into these elements from a practical point of view?

Discussion

Points (nodes), lines (networks) and areas (regions) would indeed appear to be the fundamental structure of things geographical and you will have come across studies, even in the preceding pages of this book, that incorporate all of these elements. For example, the study described in section 1.2 would involve the student finding the location of individual shops and shoppers (i.e. points), the movement patterns of shoppers (i.e. lines) and finally the trade area around individual shops (i.e. regions). Other studies, however, may not feature any of these elements particularly clearly and instead highlight an overall '*surface*'; on an OS map the contour pattern of relief is such a surface, but we can imagine similar 'isoline' maps measuring some human geographical phenomena such as environmental quality scores (see section 1.4). Reflection by the student on how isoline maps are drawn will serve to remind him or her that even a 'surface' geographical pattern is in fact based upon a sequence of point scores and we very quickly return to Smith's original simple division of geography into points, lines and areas.

From a practical point of view such a division is a useful preliminary to fieldwork because it helps us be clear about exactly what it is we wish to observe in the field. If the aim of the project is to be able to draw boundaries around areas (regions) of different characterictics, then the investigator has to be sure that the information gathered from fieldwork (which is normally expensive and time consuming and cannot be repeated very easily) is going to be sufficient or adequate for this purpose.

Smith also referred to a 'careful process of observation'. Making sense of the globe, or even a very small part of it, depends first and foremost on observation. But what constitutes 'good' observation and differentiates it from the 'bad'? Good observation is that which is more than simply subjective or personal impression. Personal impressions are often unique; in other words they usually do not coincide with or agree with those of anybody else. Personal impressions cannot be repeated by other investigators and, therefore, are useless, at least from the scientific point of view. Good observation usually implies 'objective' observation which means that other researchers undertaking the same or a similar piece of work would obtain comparable findings from his or her observations. This can be achieved by carefully selecting the *method* of observation, which is easier in some fields of inquiry than in others. When there are agreed ways to measure and universally acceptable instruments to use, then observed measurements can be quite objective (and repeatable by any number of people).

In human geography, measurement is difficult because the human geographer will never have the instrumentation that is available to the physical geography student as human behaviour does not lend itself to measurement by gadgets as precise as thermometers or barometers. Thus he or she must be aware of sources of bias or lack of precision which are major limitations of the only 'instruments' available. Generally, human geography must rely on just two types of 'instrument' for collecting primary data in the field:

1. Direct observation, in which case the investigator can be regarded as the 'instrument' as it is he or she who observes the environment, selecting the relevant parts of recording the information.

2. Questionnaire, in which case the information is extracted from people by means of a predetermined set of questions carefully designed for the specific purpose of the local study. In this case the questionnaire is the 'instrument'.

It is clearly for the investigator to decide which of these methods is most appropriate. Once this decision concerning methods has been made, the student must then evaluate which specific techniques to adopt, and in some cases other problems (such as that concerning the size of the sample of people questioned) have to be solved. The following sections discuss these practical issues more fully.

Before embarking on this discussion, however, the following simple check-list may prove useful to the student who may be considering a piece of fieldwork:

1. Do I know with some precision what information I need for my study? Have I, to the best of my knowledge, investigated all secondary sources and am I sure that the information I need is not contained in an accessible form in a published source?

2. Do I know what type of information from the field I will need? (That is to say is it information that can be observed directly or is it information that needs to be obtained from people?)

3. In the light of my answer to (2) above, can I simply undertake some kind of systematic observation or do I need to design and employ a questionnaire, or do I need a combination of both?

3.2 Observation techniques

On field *excursions*, which are a useful and often thoroughly enjoyable activity, observation is the most significant activity performed by the student. Often, the observation is guided in that an experienced geographer or someone who knows the area or the subject matter well, helps train the student's eye by picking out the key features in the landscape and encouraging accurate description. This is effective in both the urban and rural context, but it is probably in physical geography where this activity has been best developed. In physical geography the construction of the field sketch is sometimes a salutary experience as it forces the observer to concentrate hard on the underlying structure of the feature or the landscape and, for the artist and non-artist alike, sketching can be a concise way of recording observations.

However, sketching does remain primarily subjective and it is interesting that in physical geography field workers are far more inclined to *measure* slope sections, angles, the dimensions of the river channel and so on, than they once were. In a similar manner the human geographer, who may have been content to describe in words what he or she had seen, is increasingly adopting *observation techniques* in order to 'measure' more objectively the subject-matter under scrutiny.

The basic philosophy behind field observation is that the material being observed should result in essentially the same description from any number of observers. Furthermore, it is essential that the procedure for recording the information is simple, clear and readily understood and usable in the field. It is for this reason that Smith (page 43) implied that careful observation is often expressed in *numerical* form; a simple *matrix* or table can be completed easily and quickly and later is far more readily understood than endless pages of long-hand notes which may or may not be readable when the investigator comes to analyse them.

Prior to going out into the field, therefore, the investigator should plan carefully the observation procedure and if possible design some kind of observation sheet which will gradually become a data matrix as precise observations are entered on it. In order to design a suitable observation sheet, a clear *classification* of the phenomena under study must be devised. Often an existing classification can be utilised such as a classification of shops (which can be found in many urban geography books as well as in books on fieldwork techniques) or the classification of socio-economic groups as used by government agencies such as the Census of Population. Sometimes a classification has to be devised specially to suit the local area; a classification of house-types might fall into this category in order to take into account local building materials or building styles. In either case, the investigator must be quite aware that the form the classification takes is a fundamental part of the whole project as it will shape the investigation from the data collection stage to the nature of its conclusions. It must therefore be quite compatible with the aims of the project and to be confident that this is so, the investigator should wherever possible carry out a trial run or preliminary survey in order to test its validity. Very often the classification can be improved upon, as can the observation sheet, to iron out ambiguities or to take account of omissions.

Sometimes the topic under investigation may be quite abstract, such as the 'quality of life' of people living in different parts of a city. This is not to say that a classification, on which an observation sheet can be based, cannot be attempted.

Figure 3.1 attempts to show how the abstract of 'quality of life'

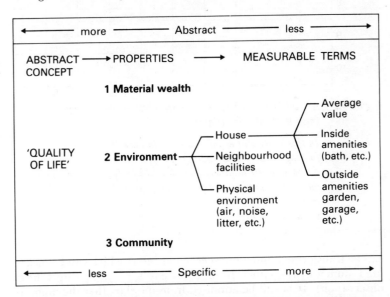

Figure 3.1   *The transformation of an abstract idea into measurable terms*

Note that the ideas become more specific and less abstract towards the right-hand side of the diagram. 'Measurable terms' have been suggested for only one of the properties that make up the concept of 'Quality of life', that is housing. (Adapted from D. M. Smith, 1975, p. 42)

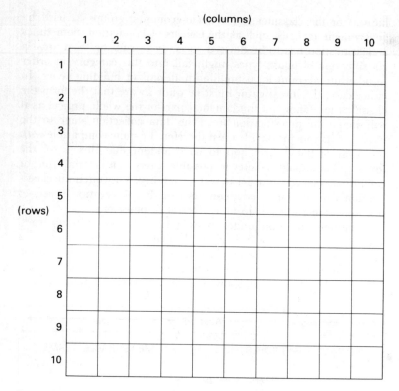

*Figure 3.2   A basic 10 × 10 matrix for recording numerical values
(measurements) in fieldwork*

> *In this particular example we would have 10 variables
> (average house value, garages etc.) which would be measured
> for each of 10 locations (which could be 'point' locations in
> the case of individual houses, small areas in the case of
> individual streets or large areas in the case of whole estates or
> wards of towns).*

can be transformed into a number of indicators which can be measured numerically (either from the Census or from direct field
observation). It has to be admitted from the start that the numerical values obtained do not give watertight and conclusive results;
they are merely indicators which, when used in combination with
each other, might give an acceptably realistic picture.

1. After examining figure 3.1, suggest additional 'properties' that
   would also serve as indicators to measure the quality of life (to
   suggest another four or five should not be too difficult).

2. Very briefly, can you complete the diagram by suggesting measurable terms that would be attainable for the other 'properties' listed and for the additional properties you have suggested?

3. After the measurable terms have been identified (or classified) for the project an observation sheet should be designed which will gradually be completed into a data matrix. Attempt to design one using figure 3.2 as an initial guide; you, as the investigator, must concentrate clearly on the *units* – both the spatial units for the rows and the variable units in the columns.

Discussion

'Quality of life' is such a wide and ill-defined concept that the range of indicator variable is also very wide. The list could include health characteristics, educational provision, leisure facilities, socioeconomic characteristics, public transport provision and so on. Some of these may be preferred to others, if only because some are more readily measured than others; 'community', for example, might prove impossible to measure with satisfactory precision, whereas leisure and recreational provision is easily observed directly. Other measurable terms might even yield to secondary sources, as 'material wealth' for example could be measured with reference to published statistics on items like car ownership per household.

To summarise, field observation needs to be mindful of the project's aims, it needs to be accurate and precise and to be clear and easily interpreted during the later stages of the investigation. For these reasons the observation sheet, based upon a well-thought-out classification of measurable objectives is the desirable tool to use; if the observer him or herself can be thought of as the instrument of measurement, then the observation sheet should be thought of as the device that 'sharpens' the instrument and improves its chances of making reliable measurements.

We have distinguished 'direct observation' from the 'questionnaire' and it is to the latter that discussion now focuses. However, the principles outlined in this section do carry over to questionnaire design and an example of a data matrix sheet is shown in figure 3.3 for which the information is not generated simply by observation but by means of a household questionnaire.

3.3 Questionnaire techniques

The design and preparation of the questionnaire are, of course, vital and the points raised in the discussion in section 3.2 about the

TRAVEL SURVEY

Home questionnaire form

We would be grateful if you would complete this form for all members of
the household aged 5 years and over.
Include all journeys made between .... and ....

Person	Sex		Age group			Occu-pation	Journey		Time		Purpose	Means
	M	F	5–11	11–18	18+		To	From	Arrive	Depart		
1												
2												
3												
4												
5												
6												
7												
8												
9												
10												
11												
12												
13												
14												
15												
16												
17												
18												
19												
20												

*Figure 3.3   Home questionnaire data sheet for recording people's travel
behaviour*

importance of classifying your objectives, defining your terms with precision and giving the procedure a trial run all remain valid in this context. There are additional points to be considered, however, largely because questionnaires deal directly with members of the public. Some of the additional points are really a matter of commonsense and others are a little more demanding, but it should be realised from the outset that the design of a reliable questionnaire is sometimes far from straightforward.

If you have ever been stopped by a student or market researcher in the street in order to answer 'a few questions' you will know that the activity does invade your privacy or at least interrupt you in whatever you are doing – shopping, meeting a friend, going to a football match, and so on. This very fact will affect your attitude to the questionnaire; you might be happy to answer the questions if you are reassured that it will not take you long, that the questions are simple to answer and that you feel that it is probably worthwhile. Thus, it is definitely bad tactics to approach people in the street – or in their homes for that matter – if the impression is given that the survey has been poorly organised, the interviewer does not seem to be sure of what he or she is doing and that there is a long list of questions for which the answers are difficult to put into few words. It is good tactics, therefore, to adopt these few pieces of good advice:

1. Have a rehearsed opening statement which is short and to the point. It should say who you are, which school or college you belong to and what the purpose of the survey is (i.e. 'a local research project' or 'for part of my examinations in geography').

2. Have a rehearsed statement which concisely explains the aim of the survey and that the anonymity of the respondent is assured.

3. State the number of questions involved, which should be very few. Four or five well-chosen questions can throw up a good deal of information. Alternatively, tell the respondent how long it will take him or her to complete the task in minutes.

4. Be efficient and courteous.

It is a matter largely of commonsense that people will not respond positively to questions that are too personal, no matter how convincing you are over your disinterest. A survey that sets out to ask householders how much they earn or how many times they have been divorced would not achieve and would not deserve success. Less serious, but still foolish, is the interviewer who asks questions on material which is easily available from published sources such as the frequency of the bus service, asks questions for which reliable answers are not likely such as on the average cost to the respondent of commuting to and from his place of work by private motor car per day.

Problems of a more philosophical nature also have to be tackled by the questionnaire designer. Possibly the fundamental problem is whether the questions should be '*open*' or '*closed*'. The former implies that the response to the question is left completely to the respondent; he or she could answer anything. For example, the answer to the question 'Where do you live?' is often left open and the respondent is encouraged to answer with his or her address. But the question could be designed so that it is 'closed', the respondent being forced to answer in one of several pre-determined ways. For example, the question 'Where do you live?' could be answered by the respondent ticking one of five statements: 0–4 miles from the town centre; 5–9 miles from the town centre; 10–19 miles from the town centre; 20–39 miles from the town centre; 40+ miles from the town centre. There are advantages and disadvantages to each method and in the example cited above the method used clearly depends upon the aim of the questionnaire; if the precise residential location of the respondent is required then obviously the 'closed' technique is inadequate. As a general rule, however, 'closed' questions are to be preferred because the responses are far easier to analyse at a later stage, although it will be clear that this type of question takes longer to prepare and that a trial run is essential so that the format can be tested. In practise a questionnaire would be expected to consist of both 'open' and 'closed' questions and a survey aiming to find out how people feel about something or to ascertain why a person behaved in one way and not another, probably cannot avoid using 'open' questions. But even in these cases the questions chosen can be designed to be as precise as possible. Care should be taken at this stage as it is beyond the competence of any local investigator to make sense of a long list of perhaps meaningless responses to questions like 'Why do you shop here?' or 'What is your opinion of this housing area?' Time invested in careful preparation is time (and frustration) saved later.

Figure 3.3 illustrates a well-designed questionnaire form. As one form is to be used for each household the address can be written on to the top of the form and then systemmatically the form completed. The number of rows required by each household will, of course, vary.

Remember that the format in figure 3.3 is not sacrosanct. In other words, depending on the precise aims of the study, the format can be adapted; for example, it may be felt that more age groupings are required if one of the primary aims of the study is to compare the mobility and transport patterns of the young and the old. This particular questionnaire utilises a combination of 'open' and

```
┌──┬──┬──┬──┐     ┌────────────────────────────────────────┐
│  │  │  │  │     │                                        │
└──┴──┴──┴──┘     └────────────────────────────────────────┘
```
....

1) This is a street plan of Bishop's Stortford. We are here. Would you mark on all the areas of open air recreation (parks etc.) which you know of, using a different colour for each area?

2) Have you personally used any of these areas within the last year?   YES ☐   NO ☐
   (if yes, please ✓ appropriate areas)

3) If answer is yes to question 2, how and how often do you use each area?

	Area:			Area:			Area:			Area:		
	tick	how freq.		tick	how freq.		tick	how freq.		tick	how freq.	
		summer	winter		summer	winter		summer	winter		summer	winter
THROUGHWAY												
TAKING CHILDREN												
SPORTS/GAMES specify												
SNACK												
WALKING DOG												
SITTING												

OTHERS (please specify) ....

4) If the Castle Gardens, Sworders Field and Grange Paddocks are:
   A) NOT used by respondent then
      a) DO YOU HAVE ANY PARTICULAR REASONS FOR NOT USING THIS AREA?
      b) If other areas are used: DO YOU HAVE ANY PARTICULAR REASONS FOR USING THESE OTHER AREAS?

a)
b)

   B) USED by respondent then:
      a) DO YOU HAVE ANY PARTICULAR REASONS FOR USING THIS AREA IN PREFERENCE TO OTHERS?
      b) DO YOU HAVE ANY REASONS FOR NOT USING THE AREA IN OTHER WAYS?

a)
b)

5) DOES ANY OTHER MEMBER OF THE HOUSEHOLD USE THE CASTLE GARDENS ... etc.? IF SO, PLEASE SAY HOW AND HOW OFTEN.

6) DO YOU OR DOES ANY MEMBER OF THE HOUSEHOLD WORK IN BISHOP'S STORTFORD?

WHERE:	OCCUPATION:

7) UNLESS YOU OBJECT, WOULD YOU PLEASE TICK THE CATEGORIES YOU AND THOSE MENTIONED ABOVE COME INTO. THANK YOU.

Age	less than 5	5–14	15–24	25–44	45–64	65 and over
Male						
Female						

Figure 3.4   Questionnaire on awareness and use of Bishop's Stortford's recreational facilities

'closed' questions and even the 'open' questions are quite precise and could be made even more precise; in the last column, entitled 'means' of transport, the expected responses could be listed, the respondent merely choosing one of them.

Compare the questionnaire shown in figure 3.3 with the more elaborate questionnaire shown in figure 3.4 which was designed by a sixth-form student. As you will see from question 1, it is designed to be used in conjunction with a street plan of the town in question, which we need not show here, although we should point out that apart from showing several street names it showed a number of well-known landmarks such as petrol stations, prominent buildings and schools. The boxes at the top of the sheet were used by the student for his or her own reference system, the address of the respondent (it was a household questionnaire) and the time and date of the interview.

1. After reading the questionnaire shown in figure 3.4, can you describe what you think the student was attempting to find out and what his initial hypothesis, or hypotheses, might have been?

2. List any sources of confusion or other weaknesses that you observe in the questionnaire, together with suggestions on how it might be improved.

3. Obviously, the entire population of the town in question cannot be interviewed. How many people and who would you ask to answer this questionnaire?

Discussion

A questionnaire ought to give a broad indication of the aims of the research and clearly the aims of the project in Bishop's Stortford was to investigate the use of the town's open air recreational facilities and the level of awareness of the townsfolk that they exist and where they are located. Question 4 attempts to find out reasons for the usage or non-usage of particular facilities and questions 6 and 7 try to extract some information about the respondents which may or may not assist in explaining the usage of the named facilities. Described in these terms the study appears to be on a fairly general level. However, the student did begin with a firm and quite precise initial idea which was stated in the form of an hypothesis. He had noticed that the Castle Gardens parkland in the town had an interesting location; it was quite central and therefore quite accessible although, owing to the alignment of a busy main road, he hypothesised that it might be 'underused'. The road separates the park physically from both residential and business areas of the town and it seemed as if the park did not enter the consciousness of workers or residents as a suitable area to use for lunch, walks, or, in the case of children, playing. His study, then, was designed to try and measure people's awareness of park space and their usage of it, and; with reference to the former; the style of question 1 is interesting; the respondent is to mark on the map with symbols the location of parks he or she knows about following a specified colour sequence (the crayons being supplied by the student). The purpose of this was to enable the student to determine the order with which respondents had remembered parks as he felt that this might be significant in later analysis.

A potential problem, although it is difficult to know how it can be solved with total success, lies in the format of question 1 in which the respondent needs to be able to read a map with relative ease and also locate items from memory – even a geography student might find this difficult sometimes! Question 4 also seems a little cumbersome and there is a danger that the questions are too open, leaving the analysis of responses potentially very difficult indeed. The problem the student faced, however, was how to state the question without 'leading' the respondent to certain answers suggested by the student.

A final comment concerns the length of the questionnaire. It would take more than just a couple of minutes to complete the questionnaire and the student would have to devote a considerable amount of his or her time to interview an adequate number of people.

On balance the questionnaire is a very bold attempt at an original and difficult project and it would be hoped that the student would offer in his or her own conclusions an assessment of how successful the questionnaire was in fulfilling its aims together with some positive suggestions on how it might be improved.

In the case of the Bishop's Stortford project, the student obtained a total of 51 successful interviews within a period of a week during the summer vacation. All questionnaire surveys, and many fieldwork projects including 'direct observation', require a *sample* to be taken as, of course, the entire population cannot be consulted. The question of how to select a sample (and how large it needs to be) is, therefore, the content of the following section.

.4 Sampling

Sampling will form an important component of many, if not the majority, of local investigations. The aim of sampling is to enable the researcher to make reliable statements about the subject matter without having to spend time and energy collecting data or measuring the entire *'population'*. Indeed sampling, when undertaken with due care and attention, is so reliable that it would usually be a waste of time to try and collect data for the whole subject-matter. Samples can be mishandled and misused and there are a number of pitfalls that the student must try to avoid falling into. These fall into two general categories:

1. The sampling procedure; how the sample is designed.
2. The interpretation of the sample results.

Both of these areas will be discussed briefly in the following pages, but first we need to be clear about the meaning of sampling. Sampling is sometimes confused with the notion of a case-study, or exemplar. A farm or a village, for instance, could be studied intensively and this would become a detailed case-study, but it would not be the same as a sample because it would not be possible to say with any measurable security that the village under study was *representative* of all villages in the area. An in-depth study of one situation is often a valid geographical study but the investigator is not justified in making general conclusions from it. A proper *sample* consists of a number of items which have been selected from the *parent population* (i.e. the whole number of items – whether they be people, households, factories or any phenomenon worthy of study). Perhaps the best known example of sampling is the 'political opinion poll' carried out at intervals by teams of professional social scientists for political parties, newspapers or television programmes, in which case the parent population is the total voting public. For example, we may read in the newspaper that the findings of an opinion poll indicate that 40 per cent of the people eligible to vote will vote Conservative, 30 per cent Labour, 20 per cent SDP/Liberal and 10 per cent 'Don't know'. Findings such as these are usually based upon a representative sample of around 1,000 people and although it is clear that we would not expect an election result to break down exactly and precisely according to the opinion poll percentages, the important fact is that the election result would reflect these percentages give or take a few percentage points. The amount of 'give or take' that needs to be allowed for can be calculated (the so-called *confidence limits* of the sample are arrived at by calculating the *standard error* of the sample mean*) and it is a comment on the reliability of sampling that political commentators and the political parties themselves take such findings very seriously indeed.

The political opinion poll example enables us to make another introductory point before we discuss sampling procedure in more

---

* The calculations required and the precise statistical context of these terms can be found in specialist texts such as *Science in Geography* (edited by B.P. Fitzgerald, OUP, 1974) and *Patterns in Human Geography* (by D.M. Smith, Penguin, 1975).

detail. The sample findings are, of course, only as good as the
actual sample. If, for example, the interviewers conducting the
survey asked people for their political opinion in only one location,
say outside Harrods in Knightsbridge, London, the results would
not be very representative of the entire British population; the
sample would have been *biased*, giving biased results. The opinion
poll researchers must ensure that a truly representative sample is
obtained, including people from various age groups, of various
social backgrounds, who live in various parts of the urban system
and in various parts of the country. Bias is always a problem in
sampling and you can never be sure that it has been eradicated
completely. The problem is minimised when the investigator adopts
a proper sampling procedure, some of which are discussed below.

The first essential task involved in preparing a sampling exercise
is to define precisely the parent population. If serious thought is
not given to this then bias might creep into your results without
you realising it. If all householders in a town are defined as the
parent population, for example, then the investigator must not
select households for interview from the telephone directory; not all
households are on the telephone and some, perhaps poorer households, would be eliminated unfairly from your study. A problem
of a similar nature arises if the parent population is 'time dependent'; traffic on the roads or pedestrian traffic in the streets would
fall into this category and the researcher would have to be careful
about when the fieldwork was undertaken as the results would
depend partly on the time of day, or the day of the week, on which
the sample was taken. In this particular case it may be desirable
to undertake several sample studies at intervals through the day
or week.

The second task is to decide upon the most appropriate sampling
method. All sampling methods have a *random* element and a clear
distinction should be made between 'random' and haphazard.
Interviewing people who you just happen to come across is not
random and such unsystematic (haphazard) methods are unlikely
to yield reliable results. In the case of a *simple random sample* the
items or observations are selected by chance, each item of the
parent population having an equal chance of being selected. This
can be done by numbering each and every item in the parent
population and selecting the desired number of items by reading
off a table of 'random numbers' (which are computer-generated
and can be found in most statistics textbooks and many books on
geographical techniques). If *points* (e.g. houses) located in space are
the items being selected then random numbers can still be used in
order to select grid coordinates and this is illustrated in figure 3.5
(a). Sometimes the investigator wishes to make a study of, say,
land-use along a *transect* through a town, in which case he or she

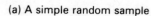

(a) A simple random sample   (b) A regular random sample

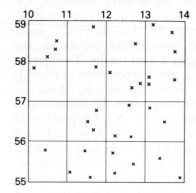   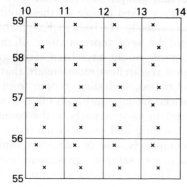

(c) A stratified random sample

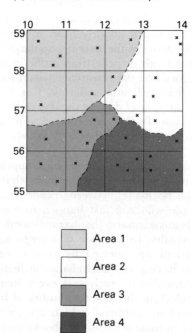

Area 1

Area 2

Area 3

Area 4

Figure 3.5   Three sampling frames

All have a random element but each may have particular strengths for particular studies.

may deliberately choose a certain route for sound reasons; however, it may be more desirable to make a study of two or three randomly chosen transect lines and these too can be selected using random numbers to select grid coordinates on the edge of the study area. These coordinates provide the points between which the transect line can be drawn. Finally, a randomly selected *area* within a region or a town can be selected in a similar way if need be.

Figures 3.5(b) and (c) illustrate two other types of sampling frame or method. They are both, in a sense, a compromise on the ideal random sample because the fundamental rule regarding equal chance of selection for each item does not apply fully. There is still a random element in each but for sound practical reasons the full randomness of the simple random sample has been reduced. It will be noticed from figure 3.5(a) that there is very patchy coverage of the whole map area. The researcher could, if he or she were unhappy about this coverage, generate a new sample and simply hope that it turned out better, but if it is essential to the study that a good spread of points (or items or areas) is selected then the researcher may decide that it would be better to have more control over the sample. Therefore, a *regular sample* may be thought more desirable than a simple random sample. Figure 3.5(b) illustrates this method for selecting, in a regular or systematic way, points in space but the same method can be used for selecting factories from a list, households or streets. The important feature is that the initial point or pattern of points is randomly selected and the regularity follows on from this random beginning.

Sometimes the very aim of the study is to compare the characteristics of different areas or regions within the study area. This could, for example, be a study of the social characteristics of people living in different housing areas within a town. Because the investigator has sub-divided the study area from the start (according to known characteristics such as house types) it means that a simple random sample and even a regular sample are both too risky because they might not select an adequate number of points from each region. Therefore, a *stratified random sample* can be instituted whereby the total population is sub-divided so that a certain number of points from each region is guaranteed. The actual points are still randomly selected. We may refer the reader back to the opinion poll example cited earlier (page 57) in which, in order to obviate bias, the survey team had to stratify the parent population (the voting public) by age group, social groups, and so on. A stratified random sample of points is illustrated in figure 3.5(c).

There now remains a third essential problem to face before the researcher actually goes into action, and this concerns the *size of the sample*. How many times need I select from the parent population in order that my results can be relied upon as being truly representative of the parent population? Commonsense tells us that the larger the sample, the more reliable it is likely to be. Statistical theory will tell us, however, that *the reliability of a sample depends simply on its size and not on its size as a proportion of the parent population.* This presents us with a slight dilemma, for although we can be reassured that our sample need not be huge even if the parent population is large, we still do not know the minimum acceptable sample size.

The short answer to this dilemma is that *the sample size should always be at least 30.* This figure is based upon statistical theory and it is certainly not the role of a book such as this to attempt to set out the necessary calculations. However, it is important that the geography student understands the proper meaning of the statement. The main implication is that after a certain minimum size (i.e. 30) diminishing returns on the reliability of the sample set in; in other words, improvement in reliability does occur for increasingly larger samples, but at an ever decreasing rate. Thus a sample consisting of say 100 interviews is not necessarily twice as good as a sample of only 50 interviews, even though it does take twice as long to complete. However, this is not to say that a sample of the minimum size of 30 is guaranteed to give reliable results; what is in fact meant is that a sample of this size is big enough for confidence limits to be calculated. In other words, a sample of less than 30 will be so unreliable that the confidence limits, even when calculated, will be meaningless.

To conclude, students should clearly aim to select a sample of at least 30 (in fact, the sample questionnaire on recreational use in Bishop's Stortford, described in the previous section on pages 52 and 53 was 51 and thus well above the minimum size). If the procedure is approached with commonsense and care, in order to reduce the problem of bias to a minimum, then a sample of this kind of size can generally be relied upon. To present findings of a sample study properly the confidence limits of the sample should be stated, otherwise the reader of the research will remain unsure about how closely the sample findings represent the parent population, or what the 'margin of error' is. This can be done in a straightforward manner by calculating the standard error of the mean, a statistic based upon probability and the normal distribution. Other texts can be consulted which give a full explanation of how this calculation is made and, more importantly, put the statistic in its proper statistical context. Examples of such texts, and there are many, include the *science in Geography* series (General Editor B.P. Fitzgerald, OUP 1974) and *Patterns in Human Geography* (D.M. Smith, Penguin, 1975).

4
. . . and back again

4.1 Sorting the wood from the trees

By the time the fieldwork part of a local studies project has been completed the investigator will be heavily involved in the topic. Refer back to figure 1.1 and you will see that at this stage the investigator is well over halfway through the normal sequence of activity. He or she has been involved in a great quantity of discussion and thought, reading and preparation, not to mention the actual work in the field. It may be at this stage the investigator feels a little overwhelmed with the notes, figures, maps, questionnaire returns and so on that have quite rapidly accumulated. The old aphorism 'I can't see the wood for the trees' takes on real meaning for the student as the initial aims of the project which seemed crystal clear at the time have become clouded and complicated by the mass of detail from the 'real world'. It is very easy to be distracted by detail which, although it might be interesting in its own right, may not be relevant or particularly useful to your specific project. In a carefully planned project this problem of irrelevant detail will possibly not arise, but the problem of coping with the information remains; 'having collected all these data, what do I do with them?'

In brief, the answer is given in figure 1.1 and table 1.1:

1. Data must be *described*.
2. Description should be accompanied by or closely followed by *analysis*.
3. Analysis could lead to *explanation*.
4. Finally it should be possible to draw *conclusions* which may be specific or general, depending on the nature of the project.

To carry our aphorism a little further we can say that *description* is the stage where the investigator cuts through the dense undergrowth and foliage so that he or she can categorise, classify and summarise what the real structure of the woodland is. That is to say, the data are manipulated so that we can see with relative ease what they reveal. *Analysis* takes this sorting procedure a stage further and the researcher tries to identify underlying relationships contained within the data which often requires him or her to establish whether initial hypotheses stated in the early stages of the project can be supported or not.

Both these stages rely on the adoption of sound and proper techniques. The purpose of this chapter is to outline some of the techniques that are available to the student in the geographical tool-bag and perhaps help the student select appropriate ones. It should be emphasised, however, that it is not the aim of this chapter to be a manual of techniques; once a specific technique of description or analysis has been selected, the student should consult specialist texts which explain the 'nuts and bolts' of the technique in proper detail.

What we are really trying to emphasise in the following pages is the problem of *selecting* techniques – whether they are appropriate for the task at hand or even whether they serve a necessary purpose at all. There is after all no point whatsoever in adopting a complex and sophisticated set of techniques if, for example, they reveal no more than was in any case self evident. Techniques are only tools and it does not matter how dazzling a technique may seem to be, it will only do its job if used properly and in the right context. It is interesting to note that even professional geographers have been duped into using complex statistical procedures which have in the end revealed little. The geography student should not also fall into this trap! As David Harvey states in the preface to his important book *Explanation in Geography* (1969):

> Not wishing to be left behind, I naturally indulged in this fashion, but found to my consternation that I only managed to accumulate a drawer full of unpublished and unpublishable papers.

Other traps also await the unwary and perhaps the most fundamental potential pitfall is to adopt a simple and elegant looking technique which is quite inappropriate owing to its lack of precision. The following example illustrates the point clearly (see figure 4.1):

The researcher in this case has arbitarily chosen five-kilometre concentric distance zones from the city centre which completely obscure the fact that there do seem to be some differences in the locational pattern of the occupational groups. If the research hypothesis was that there are significant differences between the location of surgeons and bricklayers within the town then this cartographic technique lacks the precision to make any realistic comment.

Simplistic though this example is, it does make the point clearly. Techniques of description and analysis are to help clarify and reveal. Used thoughtlessly and aimlessly they will only serve to obscure what is really important.

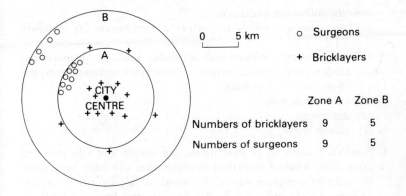

Figure 4.1 The location of two occupational groups

> *A hypothetical distribution which has been analysed by
> distance zone from the city centre. The table displaying the
> results of this analysis show the distribution of the two
> occupational groups to be identical. The map shows that the
> technique is far too crude and is wholly inappropriate.*

4.2 Description

Geography has always had an important function to describe land-
scapes and regions and in thc past some geographers became
admired for their literary accomplishments as they were able, in
words, to relate the 'feel' and character of places almost to the same
pitch as great 'regional' novelists such as Arnold Bennett. Careful
choice of words and accurate, unambiguous English are of prime
importance, but when much of the researcher's information has
been collected in numerical form there are other more appropriate
techniques which can be used in addition to plain words:

1. Carefully assembled tables of data.

2. Graphical techniques; bar charts, line graphs, pie diagrams and
   other more specific graphs, such as the Lorenz Curve can each
   serve a useful role.

3. Maps are the tools which are by definition specially geographical as they focus on the spatial dimension, showing spatial
   distributions of phenomena. They can be divided into the 'qualitative', which show 'what is there' as in the case of OS maps,
   and the 'quantitative' which show the distribution of some measured quantity as in the case of a map showing pedestrian den-
   sities, for example. Quantitative maps can be further sub-divided

into the following main types:
(a) maps using symbols to portray a distribution (as in figure 4.1);
(b) maps using proportional symbols, such as proportional circles, proportional arrows to show flows or movements, pie charts and bar graphs;
(c) choropleth maps;
(d) dot maps;
(e) isoline maps.

4. Statistical methods of description are simple and effective and often some kind of statistical manipulation will have been done in order to complete any of the items in (a), (b) or (c) above. Descriptive statistics can be divided into two broad groups:
(a) measures of central tendency or the average: the mode, the median and the mean;
(b) measures of spread or variation: the standard deviation and the range.

One important function of the description stage is 'communication' by which we mean that it is one objective of the student to ensure that information that he or she believes to be significant is 'put over' in the most direct and accessible manner. This often necessitates a combination of descriptive techniques being used and this can be illustrated by the following example:
Data on 'material wellbeing' were obtained at ward level for the whole of the city of Newcastle-upon-Tyne, with the object of investigating the spatial pattern of material wealth in the city. One of the indicators of material wealth chosen was the ownership of deep freezes per household. For the researcher there were two initial questions that the data needed to answer:

1. Was the distribution of deep freezes even or uneven?

2. If the distribution was uneven, which areas of the city were better off than average and which were worse off?

With this very brief outline of the project, attempt to answer the following questions for yourself:

1. Do you think data such as these were obtained by the student by direct observation, questionnaire or from secondary sources? Justify your answer.

2. List the possible ways in which the data could be described and presented.

3. In addition to the data on deep freezer ownership, what else would you need in order to answer the questions the student had posed for herself?

4. Are there any advantages in using more than one descriptive technique in this particular case?

Discussion

It is most unlikely, of course, that a student would have the time or the resources to obtain data such as these from sources other than secondary sources. In fact, household consumption data is available from the local authority offices in the city of Newcastle-upon-Tyne in a publication called *Urban Trends*. The data are presented in tabular form in the source, but from the point of view of 'communication' and in the light of the students stated objectives, merely to reproduce the table in a local studies report would be most inadequate. A table is sometimes difficult to absorb especially when it contains large figures and there are better ways for the student to communicate what she believes to be significant. Figure 4.2(a) shows the data transformed into a Lorenz Curve which compares the actual evenness of the distribution to the theoretical 'perfectly even distribution' (the 45° line); the more the actual curve deviates away from the 45° line the less even is the distribution. Note that the student had to obtain *population* data at ward level as well as deep freezer ownership data in order to draw this graph. In addition, the student needed a ward map of Newcastle in order to answer the second of her questions; the data was divided into a number of class grouping and then mapped using the choropleth method (figure 4.2(b)). In view of the students stated objectives neither the map nor the Lorenz Curve is an adequate descriptive device on its own. The limitations of the Lorenz Curve are probably clear as it does not show the actual distribution in space. What it does do is graphically illustrate the degree of unevenness of the distribution, and, although the map does do this in a sense, the impact, it may be argued, is far less immediate. The two techniques together compliment each other well.

At this point it would be worthwhile to draw attention to a number of simple but, nevertheless, important issues. Figure 4.3 is a redrawn version of a map presented by a student using the same source of data from Newcastle-upon-Tyne as discussed above. It would be a worthy and perhaps timely exercise to ask yourself what the *defects* of this map are, which have in fact devalued it into something little more than useless. Defects noted by the authors include:

1. The title is vague. The consumption of what? Does the title imply one indicator variable has been used, or have a number of different ones been combined to form one composite index?

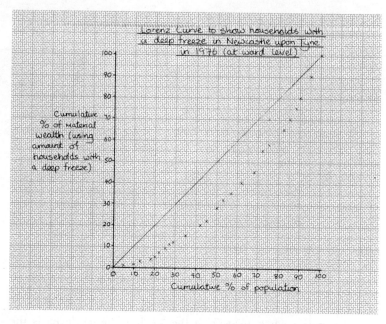

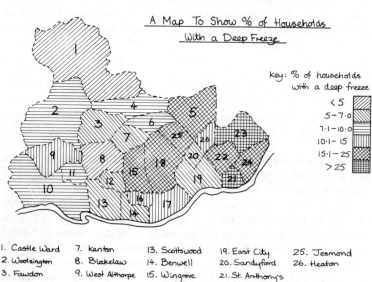

A Map To Show % of Households
With a Deep Freeze

key: % of households
with a deep freeze

< 5
5 – 7.0
7.1 – 10.0
10.1 – 15
15.1 – 25
> 25

1. Castle Ward	7. Kenton	13. Scotswood	19. East City	25. Jesmond
2. Woolsington	8. Blakelaw	14. Benwell	20. Sandyford	26. Heaton
3. Fawdon	9. West Althorpe	15. Wingrove	21. St. Anthony's	
4. Gosforth 2	10. New Burn	16. Elswick	22. St. Lawrence	
5. Dene	11. Denton	17. West City	23. Walkergate	
6. Gosforth 1	12. Fenham	18. Moorside	24. Walker	

Figure 4.2   Lorenz Curve and choropleth map presented by a student for part of a local studies project in Newcastle-upon-Tyne

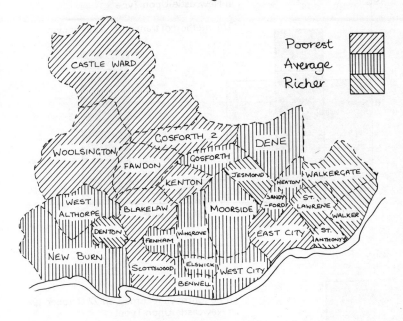

Figure 4.3   An exact copy of a map presented by a student as part of a local studies project

2. The key does not help us as there is no reference to any units. If the data have been transformed into an index, then there are no units, but the key should offer an explanation.

3. Finally, the map suffers from a lack of careful presentation. Simply, a scale and a frame would improve matters.

A final general word on data description would emphasise the importance of proper and full *use* of the various techniques available. For example, if more than one distribution needs to be shown on a map, and it is important to compare the two distributions, then tracing paper overlays can be very useful indeed. But on a more basic level than this, examine figure 4.4 which consists of two bar graphs which are also exact copies from a student's work. Once again, it would be a worthwhile exercise to identify the weaknesses of these graphs. They are large and imposing diagrams which, while in itself not a terribly important drawback, rather serves to highlight their simplicity. Would it not be as effective, if not *more* effective, to present the data in the form of a neat table or matrix? This is especially so in this particular case as the vertical axes, though obvious after a second or two of thought, are not labelled

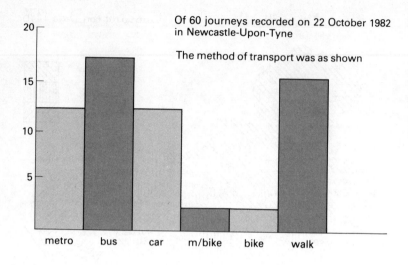

Of 60 journeys recorded on 22 October 1982 in Newcastle-Upon-Tyne

The method of transport was as shown

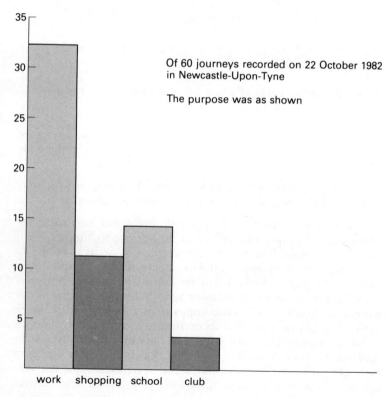

Of 60 journeys recorded on 22 October 1982 in Newcastle-Upon-Tyne

The purpose was as shown

Figure 4.4

or given units. If the researcher believes that a diagram is required then it should be designed a little better and, more importantly, tell us something more; for example, the graph showing transport methods could easily be added to, to show us the proportion of the sample using public transport as opposed to private modes. The reader could think of other small improvements such as this (the data were collected in the form shown by the questionnaire sheet on page 50, figure 3.3, and reference to this sheet will help you).

4.3 Analysis. . . and explanation?

'Explanation', which can sometimes arise out of sound analysis, is the most difficult part of any geographical study. We must be sure that we understand its meaning.

Essentially, when we attempt to explain something in geography we are trying to find reasons. It has been put in a simple though rather neat way in the following 'definition' of geography. Geography, it has been said, answers the following composite question: 'What is where and why?' The 'what' and the 'where' questions are a matter for accurate description and it is the 'why' question that seeks to offer explanation (sometimes supplemented with a 'how' question as well). Now, this might seem a perfectly straightforward distinction but there does remain a potential trap that can catch out the unaware student. Smith writes in the epilogue to his book *Patterns in Human Geography* (1975, pp. 347–348):

> The distinction between description and explanation has been stressed a number of times in the previous pages. A critical question in geography is the extent to which pattern might suggest process, or the links of cause and effect which lead things to be as they are. To identify and describe a pattern is not necessarily to know the process at work. The nature of a pattern might imply something of the process – that it makes for dispersal or concentration, or that it leads to regularity of spatial arrangement rather than clustering or randomness. But a nearest neighbour statistic . . . . . . explains nothing in itself.

The point we wish to make is that it is easy to assume mistakenly that explanation has been found once the *pattern* has been adequately described. It is true that sometimes this is as far as the project can go, as to determine the real *process* may be way beyond the scope of the project. This can be illustrated with reference to figure 4.5 which shows an isoline map which describes the results of an environmental quality survey based upon an observation sheet not unlike the one shown in table 1.2. You can ask yourself whether the map and the procedure leading up to its compilation offers any

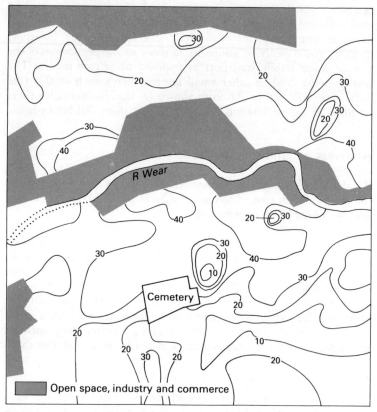

*Figure 4.5   Isoline map of 'Environmental Scores' based upon an
environmental quality survey undertaken by students at
Sunderland Polytechnic*

explanation; indeed, you might ask, explanation of what? The valid
aims of this piece of work were to develop a difficult field technique –
measuring a qualitative part of the environment using a quantitative technique – and an attempt to describe the pattern of
environmental quality within the city. It may offer some 'explanation' in the sense that the field observation sheets will have
recorded 'why' some areas score differently from other areas, but
this, of course, is not real explanation; to say that a certain area
of the city if deprived because it has bad housing, for example, does
not give the reasons for the deprivation.

In order to reinforce our argument we may refer to the results of
some very famous pieces of research in urban geography (which
incidentally were not undertaken by geographers, as figure 4.6
shows). Most students of urban geography can reproduce the

Model	Burgess	Hoyt	Harris and Ullman
Country of origin	USA	USA	USA
Date of publication	1925	1939	1945
Academic discipline	Human ecology	Land economics	Sociology
Focus	Social & ethnic groups	Property values	Urban activities, social groups
Status (inductive or deductive)	Deductive	Inductive	Deductive
Processes specified within the model	Immigration, urban expansion, invasion & succession	Urban expansion	Attraction & repulsion
Resulting pattern:			

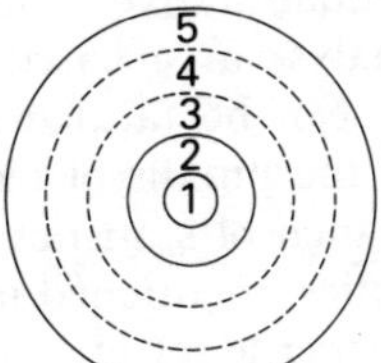

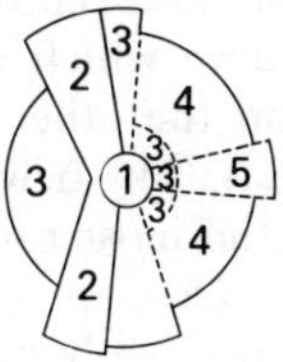

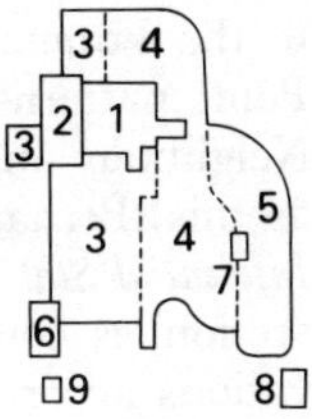

Figure 4.6   Models in urban geography

pattern of Burgess's 'rings', Hoyt's 'sectors' or Harris and Ullman's 'multiple nuclei', but tests show that comparatively few can successfully explain the processes that the research workers had identified as those resulting in the well-known patterns described by the models. As figure 4.6 very briefly summarises each model has a different focus of attention and concentrates on different urban processes, Hoyt being firmly based in economic processes and the other two being more concerned with aspects of sociology. In all cases the pattern of the model serves a useful purpose in giving us a simplified picture summary, but in many ways it is the least important part of the research as the aim of the research was to provide some real explanation.

This important discussion should remind the student that explanation is often subtle and very hard to find and it may well be that many individual local investigations cannot realistically aspire to this level. Description, as we have seen, does not explain a process, and, although rigorous analysis can lead to explanation, it need not necessarily do so.

The *purpose of analysis* is to examine the evidence in order to seek regularities and relationships within it. The list of techniques given in the previous section is relevant in this context because by carefully describing the data in tabular, graph, cartographic or statistical form can perform useful initial analysis. The boundary between description and analysis is, in this sense, very blurred and constructing a Lorenz Curve, for example, can be said to have performed both functions. Compiling a series of maps, or a map with a number of overlays, again not only describes the results of a field survey but assists in highlighting spatial regularities in the data or even relationships between two or more sets of data.

In the field of statistics, however, the tool-bag can be usefully added to, enabling further analysis. There are, for example, specific techniques that have been developed in order to analyse geographical distribution of various kinds. The Location Quotient and Coefficient of Localisation are quantitative techniques related to the Lorenz Curve which can analyse area based distributions. Point patterns, on the other hand, can be tackled using Nearest Neighbour analysis (but beware of the pitfalls of techniques such as this).Perhaps the most useful branch of statistics is the area of *Inferential Statistics*. Descriptive statistics, mentioned in the previous section, is concerned with summarising a set of numerical observations according to given rules, whereas inferential statistics sets out to infer relationships between sets of observations. For the geography student there are perhaps two techniques which are particularly prominent, these being the chi-square test and tests of correlation (most notably the Spearman's rank correlation coefficient). In either case it is important that the student approaches the test in a formal way and conducts it according to the method explained in a specialist text book.

The chi-square test enables the researcher to compare the frequency distribution of two sets of observations. It compares a set of 'observed frequencies' with a set of 'expected frequencies' and establishes the probability that the differences in the observed frequencies resulting merely by chance. This is useful because it enables the researcher to determine whether the difference he or she has observed between some measured characteristic of two housing estates, farms or villages is large enough to be considered 'significant'. If the difference is not statistically significant, it could well have simply occurred by chance (or sampling error) and the researcher is, therefore, clearly not justified in attempting to seek explanations for his or her observations.

Among the most widely used statistical method in geography is the correlation technique which analyses whether two sets of observations are statistically related to each other, whether in a negative or positive manner. The coefficient will vary from −1 (perfectly negative) through 0 (no correlation at all) to +1 (perfectly positive) and tables can be consulted to determine the 'significance' of the coefficient; whether or not a result is statistically significant is, of course, vital as inferences about the relationship between two sets of data cannot be made safely on the grounds of a weak correlation. In the light of our earlier discussion in this section an important distinction must be made between a statistically significant relationship and the use of this to infer a *causal relationship* (or explanation). There is a difference between the discovery of a relationship which enables us to make *predictions* of one of the variables based upon observations of the other, and those that demonstrate an explanation – that one variable is *caused* by the other. Prediction is usually easier than explanation and the two should not be confused. For example, there is often a strong positive correlation to be found between land values in the CBD of a large town and the density of pedestrian traffic; does this mean that one causes the other, or is there some other separate explanation for each variable?

True explanations are hard to find and even the most thoroughly researched projects do not often reach this summit of achievement. If a project can show that a predictable relationship exists (or not), a certain regularity can be found (or not) or simply define some new questions that ought to be asked then the work will probably have proved worthwhile.

5
Field investigation as an examined topic

Increasing numbers of students present a written report of their local investigation as part of their examination at 'A' level. A well-presented report will contain a discussion on each of the stages outlined in figure 1.1 although, of course, each stage does not merit equal space in the report. Perhaps the most important, though by no means the longest, element is the conclusion, which should aim to be clear, concise and explicit. If the research does not yield the evidence to support a definite final statement or to substantiate the initial hypothesis then the project can often end on a positive note by making suggestions on how the method could be improved upon and by proposing promising lines of further research. A report should never merely 'fade away', remaining inconclusive and vague; and remember that negative results can be every bit as useful and worthwhile as positive results.

As a conclusion to this book we can present two types of information concerning this very practical aspect of field investigation relating to examinations. These are:

1. Examiners' comments, sometimes made to students soon after they first submit their project title. The aim of these comments is to help the student in his or her deliberations on approaches and methods.

2. More general statements made by examination boards and examiners on the nature of what they consider to be good practice which, of course, is the basis for producing a good piece of work.

Consider the following titles along with the accompanying examiner's comment (which are returned by the examiner before the student begins his or her work in earnest).

Title: (submitted by student)	Comment: (returned by examiner)
Does East Hertfordshire suffer from 'rural deprivation'?	Questionnaires need much care with sampling framework and form of questions to get reliable results. A pilot run with it may

Title: (submitted by student)	Comment: (returned by examiner)
	be needed. The candidate seems interested to identify *areas* as well as groups who suffer deprivation. The two may be interlinked and the second will be more difficult to pin down – what may appear deprivation to one old person may not appear so to another and one wonders how Ian will allow for this. Clearly he will have to map the distribution of services in relation to where people live to find areas poorly served by doctors, buses etc. but he needs to use a wide range of such services and recognise that not all people need all services.
An attempt to measure externality fields in Cambridge using housing data.	One wonders why the candidate will use house prices to correlate with his externalities since house prices will be influenced by a wide range of other more important factors, such as the character and quality of the house itself. Why not use rateable values for *selected* house types which should be more accessible and might also reflect these externalities. Much care will be needed in assessing good and bad externalities – don't assume that all factories, for example, are equally bad neighbours.
An investigation into the awareness and use of Bishop's Stortford's recreational facilities.	A very difficult topic as asking questions on people's perception contains many pitfalls whilst mapping people's use of recreational area depends on much repeated observation to get a reasonable view of the situation. Should the candidate tie it down

Title: (submitted by student)

Comment: (returned by examiner)

more to ask people at selected locations in the town, for example, to mark on a map the main open-air recreational sites, as well as asking them how they use them, to see if awareness of this park is rather local to it; compared with other parks?

An investigation into the 'neighbourhood principle' in Stevenage New Town, with special reference to retailing.

Should one base a study on the analysis of only one service (retailing) since the New Town neighbourhood principle implies more than that? Also the character of retailing is largely out of the hands of planners – they just provide the shops, private enterprise determines the types of shops – whereas the location of schools etc. is determined by the 'planners'. Perhaps more should be done with these.

What were health conditions like in the late nineteenth-century Bishop's Stortford?

An interesting topic so long as the records that the candidate plans to use are detailed enough, at least for selected years, to allow him to compose maps of the town that may show distribution of health characteristics. Don't let it become merely an account of sanitation and water supply improvements etc. for the whole town, unless again spatial variations within the town can be identified.

When the student submits his or her title, it is accompanied by a 100 or so word outline of the project. Writing such a brief summary of aims and methods is a very useful exercise indeed as it concentrates the mind.

1. The students' outlines have not been presented here. In the light of the examiner's comments, however, take one of the five titles and write a carefully worded statement of aims and methods of the project.

2. This is a skill that improves with practice. You may wish to attempt a similar summary with several other titles. Remember, the clearer this stage is, the easier following stages in the project become.

3. Exchange your outlines with a fellow student and play the role of the examiner; try to add a comment or two to the existing examiner's comment.

Selecting and then clarifying the title is the first crucial stage in executing a local studies project. What is required in the following stages might best be illustrated with reference to examination board guidelines.

In assessing 'A' level fieldwork projects, the Joint Matriculation Board, for example, uses a five-point grading system which, when revised in 1976, became rather more precise as table 5.1 shows.

Table 5.1   Grading system used by the Joint Matriculation Board in the assessment of 'A' level fieldwork.

1968	1976
1. Quality of observation	1. Statement of aims and relevance of material
2. Evidence of field techniques used	2. Quality of observation and records
3. Evidence of reasoning	3. Evidence of field techniques used
4. Relevance of material	4. Use of data and relevance of material
5. Quality, use, relevance and integration of illustrations	5. Quality, use, relevance and integration of illustrations and secondary source material

Source: J. Alan Taylor, 1977

The Associated Examination Board, on the other hand, give in their syllabus document advice for supervisors of fieldwork project on how projects are to be assessed. It forms a seven-point plan although it is remarkably similar to the Joint Matriculation Board scheme:

1 Clear statement of aims and objectives of the work carried out
2 Methods of investigation and collection of data

3 Relevance and quality of the skills and techniques applied to the data
4 Relevance, interpretation and use of information collected
5 Conclusions reached
6 Originality and individuality of the report
7 Presentation, cohesion and logical development

It is worthwhile to try and relate these points to the step-by-step approach adopted in this book, although the student must bear in mind that in so far as *techniques* of data description and analysis are concerned the more specialist text books should be consulted.

As a final word it is worth quoting from the Associated Examination Board syllabus document on the wider benefits of individual local investigation (1982, p. 11):

> Fieldwork is considered an essential component in the education of a geographer for the following reasons:
> 1. geography is both a theoretical and practical subject and a full understanding of the subject may be accomplished through undertaking fieldwork investigation;
> 2. geography has become an increasingly applied subject, giving rise to the need to relate geographical studies to wider problems of social and scientific interest;
> 3. field investigations afford candidates the opportunity to work independently or to accept individual responsibility within a group investigation.

Thus, successful field research undertaken by the student can provide a very firm foundation for his or her examination; and, more than this, the above comment implies that it would be impossible to envisage a properly educated 'geographer' not having been involved with the local environment firsthand. Furthermore, it is our contention that field research can be great fun and deeply rewarding.

Photographic section

1 Behind closed doors

Much information that is of interest to the geographer has to be sought out. This is not that it is obscure, only that at first it may be concealed from view. These houses present some self-evident information – about their ages, styles, states of repair and so on. Less obvious but perhaps more interesting are questions such as who lives in them? What is the size of households? What are their leisure time activities? And so on.

Thus housing is a very rich seam for geographical study, but the main practical question for the researcher is '*How* do I obtain the information I need?'

2 Every face is a picture

And every picture tells a story. The subject matter in human geography is infinite as each person's experience is unique and the ways people interact is also very wide ranging. But having said this it is also true that *groups* of people tend to behave in predictable ways, and it is the study of the resulting *general* patterns, and the processes that are responsible for them, that allows the researcher to make progress.

Study the photograph which shows that it would be a hopeless task to study each individual's migratory experience, for example, and then try to gain some kind of understanding of migration by comparing each unique case study. However it is quite practical to take a group of this size (or greater) and study averages, tendencies, significant differences between sub-groups, correlations of variables, etc.

An important practical problem facing the researcher is the classification of data. How many ways can you subdivide the collection of people in this photograph?

3 Big Brother is watching?

Despite certain predictions made about 1984, we are not in the situation of being continually monitored by a vast computerised system, the information it stores being available at the touch of a button. But the researcher should not forget, especially in the early stages of a study, that there is much information in a secondary form freely available to those with the energy and initiative to delve into libraries and archives to obtain it.

The most up-to-date and complete data set for the British population is the 1981 census. The photograph shows some of the publicity material distributed during the run-up to census night, designed to explain the aims of the census to the public. To explain an exercise like this fully is, of course, desirable as it increases the trust of people and increases their ability to answer the questions accurately. This point should not be lost to the researcher conducting his or her own survey.

4 'Excuse me ... '

Many students have had this kind of active fieldwork experience before entering the sixth form. However, when you are totally responsible for the design of the questions, selecting the sample and all the other jobs, it feels, and indeed is, a major undertaking. There are several traps for the unwary which, if not avoided, may seriously weaken a study. It is a good idea to make a list of these before embarking on the task.

5 'This is the way it is'

The picture here depicts what is sometimes referred to as traditional fieldwork, and it should not be underrated; you can learn much by 'being there', listening to the teacher who knows the area and has the expertise to interpret, offer advice and suggest explanations.

Apart from in the initial planning stages of individual fieldwork, the student cannot expect this sort of close guidance. He or she must develop his or her own expertise in choosing and operating field techniques.

6 Technology takes over

This is becoming a common scene, almost a cliché, in last quarter of the twentieth century. There is no doubt that computers will be of great assistance to students for information retrieval and data processing. Many projects however will not require computing facilities and this scene, person and machine in harmony, will not be appropriate. However, the illustration helps us make the vital point for the reader of this book; that the book is not a technical manual and it is not filled with template fieldwork exercises that the student may simply copy. The whole emphasis is to encourage the student toward good geography of his or her own – which may or may not involve computers or any of the other specific tools and techniques.

Photograph 1   Behind closed doors

Photograph 2   Every face is a picture

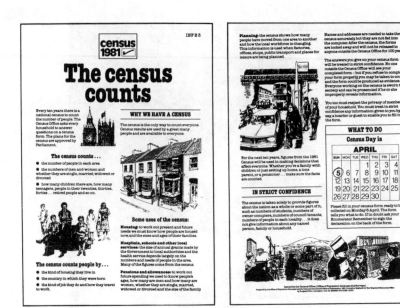

Photograph 3   Big Brother is watching?

Photograph 4 'Excuse me...'

Photograph 5   'This is the way it is'

Photograph 6   *Technology takes over*

References

Associated Examining Board, Wellington House, Aldershot, Hampshire, GU11 1BQ.

Chisholm, M., (1975), *Human Geography: evolution or revolution?*, Penguin, Harmondsworth.

Hancock, J., (1980), *Urban Development and Planning*, Basil Blackwell, Oxford.

Harvey, D., (1969), *Explanation in Geography*, Arnold, London.

Hertfordshire Structure Plan (1976), The Chief Executive, H.C.C. County Hall, Hertford, SG13 8DN.

Herts '71, part of MicroQUERY package from the Advisory Unit for Computer Based Education, Endymion Road, Hatfield, Hertfordshire, AL10 8AU.

Parry, G., (1981), 'Census shows drift out of towns', *Guardian*, 30 June 1981.

Pacione, M., (1981), 'The Cognitive-behavioural Approach to Urban Studies', *Teaching Geography*, **6**(4) pp. 186–9.

Short, J.R., (1980), *Urban Data Sources*, Butterworth, London.

Smith, D.M., (1975), *Patterns in Human Geography*, Penguin, Harmondsworth.

Taylor, J.A., (1977), 'Examining A-level fieldwork', *Teaching Geography*, **3**(1), pp. 12–13.

University of Cambridge Local Examinations Syndicate, Syndicate Buildings, 17 Harvey Road, Cambridge, CB1 2EU.